American M
Physicians dedicated t(

MW01057174

Financial

Management

of the Medical Practice

Second Edition

Max Reiboldt, CPA
The Coker Group

Practice Success Series

Financial Management of the Medical Practice
Second Edition

Additional copies of this book may be ordered by calling 800 621-8335. Mention product number OP701102.

ISBN 1-57947-291-5

Library of Congress Cataloging-in-Publication Data

Reiboldt, J. Max
   Financial management of the medical practice / Max Reiboldt.-- 2nd ed.

      p. cm.
      ISBN 1-57947-291-5
   1. Medicine--Practice--Finance. I. American Medical Association. II.
   Coker Group. III. Title.
      R728 .R445 2002
      610'.65'0681--dc21

                                        2002009655

BQ13:02-P-041:09/02

The Coker Group, a leader in health care consulting, helps providers attain improved financial and operational results through sound business principles. The consulting team members are proficient, trustworthy professionals with experience and strengths in various areas. The well-rounded staff includes individuals seasoned in finance, administration, management, operations, compliance, personnel management, and information systems.

The Coker Group's nationwide client base includes major health systems, hospitals, physician groups, and solo practitioners in a full spectrum of engagements. The Coker Group has gained a reputation since 1987 for thorough, efficient, and cost-conscious work to benefit its clients financially and operationally. The firm has a towering profile with recognized and respected health care professionals throughout the industry. The Coker Group's exceptional consulting team has health care, technical, financial, and business knowledge and offers comprehensive programs, services, and training to yield long-term solutions and turnarounds. Coker staff members are devoted to delivering reliable answers and dependable options so that decision-makers can make categorical decisions. Coker consultants enable providers to concentrate on patient care.

Service Areas

- Practice management, billing and collection reviews, chart audits
- Procedural coding analysis
- Information systems review, including EMR
- Physician employment and compensation review
- Physician network development
- Practice appraisals
- Strategic planning/business planning
- Disengagements of practices and network unwinds
- Practice operational assessments
- Contract negotiations
- Hospital services, medical staff development
- Practice start-ups
- Buy/sell and equity analysis
- Sale/acquisition negotiations
- Group formation and dissolution
- Educational programs, workshops, and training
- Compliance plans
- HIPAA assessments and compliance
- MSA development

- Financial analysis
- Mediation and expert witnessing
- Policies and procedures manuals

For more information, contact:

The Coker Group

11660 Alpharetta Hwy/Suite 710/Roswell, GA 30076

800.345.5829 www.cokergroup.com

Max Reiboldt, Managing Partner, CEO of The Coker Group, based in Atlanta, Georgia, has been greatly involved with medical practice consulting since 1992. During this period, he has experienced first hand the incredible changes within the business of medical practice.

With over 10 years of extensive work with physicians and health systems, combined with 29 years' experience across multiple industries, Mr Reiboldt knows what motivates physicians and what sustains the motivation of physicians who transition from ownership of a practice to employment by the practice. He also knows what health systems need to maintain their viability in a highly competitive market. His work, which includes the development of physician compensation plans in integrated health care systems, uniquely qualifies him to work effectively with organizations of all sizes.

Mr Reiboldt is a popular speaker at practice management seminars and workshops where physician leaders and health system administrators gather to learn how to cope in the rapidly changing health care market. Frequently engaged to speak by professional associations and pharmaceutical companies, Mr Reiboldt has a keen knowledge of managed care's effects on medical practice management. He is proficient in employing practical responses to the fiscal realities of market demands.

Mr Reiboldt has been a major contributor to the AMA Press series of books on practice management, *PRACTICE SUCCESS!* Titles specifically attributed to Mr Reiboldt include *Physician Compensation Systems, Financial Management of the Medical Practice, Assessing the Value of the Medical Practice,* and *Buying, Selling, and Owning the Medical Practice.* Other published works by Mr Reiboldt include a management series for independent physician associations with the McGraw-Hill Healthcare Education Group. In 2001, Reiboldt co-authored *Beyond Disengagement: Recreating the Physician Practice,* published by AMA Press.

As managing partner of The Coker Group, Mr Reiboldt engages in consulting projects with physicians and health systems nationwide. His expertise covers practice acquisition negotiations, MSO administration and planning, primary care network development, independent physician group formation, practice consultations, compliance issues, integrated delivery systems formation, practice operational assessments, physician compensation plan design, and practice brokering.

Mr Reiboldt is licensed as a certified public accountant by the states of Georgia and Louisiana, and is a member of the American Institute of Certified Public Accountants, the Healthcare Financial Management Association, and the American Society of Appraisers.

The typical twenty-first century medical practice is a multi-million dollar business operation that handles the livelihood of many people, along with the health care of scores of lives. Fiscal responsibility is mandatory—not optional—to compete and survive in a challenging health care environment.

An important aspect of medical practice management, or a similar health care entity, is monitoring the finances of the organization. Typically, those who are responsible are generalists or administrators with broad skill sets in business operations, not accountants or financial managers. Monitoring and observing historical and current data allows the administrator to make informed decisions, or in other cases, to communicate important financial information to those who are decision-makers for the practice.

Financial management of the medical practice encompasses gathering data, interpreting data, and appropriately responding. Financial management comes from various roles within the practice, with responsibilities spanning numerous job descriptions. Some tasks and oversight will be at the administrative level, while other responsibilities will be at the ownership level. The savvy manager will understand the nuances of data, the information that it yields, and the applications that must be made to achieve a viable business organization.

The purpose of this book is to help management generalists and administrators attain a sufficient level of understanding of the financial aspects of practice management so that they may successfully function in this position. Filled with charts, checklists, examples, and sample reports, this book presents the necessary tools and fundamentals to assist the management generalists and administrators in their position.

The author recognizes that the administrator of the practice may or may not have formal accounting training, hold a position of ownership, and be the ultimate decision-maker in the practice. The objective of this book is to provide foundational information to nonfinancial managers that can be enhanced or supported by accounting professionals who are selected to serve the practice. With a strong foundation, the practice administrator or management generalists' role will provide the practice with sound operational processes and fiscal stability.

CONTENTS

chapter 1

Reporting Standards of the Practice

The practice of reporting financial information as a function in today's operation of a medical practice is particularly important due to intense demands for fiscal acuity. As practices mature, requirements for sound financial management increase. To meet these demands, medical practices, both physician-owned and health system-owned, must adhere to advanced, organized, and accurate reporting standards.

This chapter explores the basic concepts that are key to understanding financial statements for the medical practice. In addition, the main areas of reporting and compilation of financial statements are reviewed.

UNDERSTANDING FINANCIAL STATEMENTS

Understanding financial statements is based on four areas of importance:

- Understanding the theories
- Understanding the purpose
- Understanding the practicality
- Understanding the effect

Understanding the Theories

Financial management of most medical practices does not require an accounting degree or specialized training. Although larger health care entities and hospital-owned networks may require a designated chief financial officer, advanced knowledge of accounting theory is not as important for smaller practices. The following basic theories will assist the average medical practice with its financial management needs:

- **Outline of accounts.** Keep a detailed list of all accounts, including asset accounts, liability accounts, and equity and income statement accounts. Account inquiry is important to the accountant or bookkeeper who must appropriately and accurately depict the transactions as required by accounting protocol. Ultimately, these accounts are reflected in the financial statements. The physician-owner or nonaccounting administrator should grasp the "big picture" — not become bogged down in the minutia of the numbers. Financial interpretation calls for the application of common sense and intellectual reasoning to override many areas that, in accounting, appear as "black and white," when in reality they are "gray."

■ **Cash-based versus accrual-based accounting.** The non-accounting manager of a medical practice must understand the difference between cash-based accounting and accrual-based accounting.

   ■ **Cash-based accounting.** This type of accounting calls for the recognition of revenue when money is received and recognition of an expense when payment is made.

   ■ **Accrual-based accounting.** This type of accounting considers revenue when it is earned and expense when it is incurred.

As a matter of accounting theory, accrual-based accounting is more accurate, a better gauge of a medical practice's performance, and more applicable for larger practices. For smaller practices, cash-based accounting is more relevant and easier to understand by the nonaccountant business owner.

Although cash-based accounting may not be as technically accurate, it can be mitigated when practices are promptly paying their liabilities, thus, closely reflecting payment with services rendered. Revenue is not matched as easily when comparing cash-based versus accrual-based accounting because most medical practices and other health care entities receive the greater part of services-rendered monies somewhat later from a third-party insurer or payer.

In choosing an appropriate accounting method for a practice, both a practical and relevant approach must be used:

■ Cash-based accounting is preferred for small businesses, such as medical practices with less than ten providers.

■ Accrual-based accounting is required for larger health care entities due to its greater accuracy and for consolidation purposes. Larger entities generally are subject to scrutiny of their operations by outside members, investors, and management leaders, including boards of directors.

Even larger entities under accrual-based accounting should assume cash reporting responsibilities so that management will also be able to review that performance. As in most businesses, cash flow is the most important factor for near- or long-term survival. Therefore, to maintain accurate and timely cash accounting, reporting is essential, regardless of whether a cash-based or accrual-based method of accounting is used.

Understanding the Purpose

The purpose of financial statements and other financial data is to allow the owners and managers of the business to properly reflect upon what has happened so that they can have an influence on the future. It is gratifying to reflect upon a successful month, quarter, or year, but kudos for past performances does little toward assuring a successful future. Reflective analysis of financial information (ie, through the review of a financial statement) should be used primarily to determine what could be done to improve operations in the future.

Key employees, department heads, and other staff members should take part in reviewing the financial statement. All managers should have a sufficient level of understanding so that they can interpret the practice's overall performance as they interact with subordinates and superiors.

The purpose of the financial statement is to provide key personnel the opportunity to react to certain decisions as they relate to ongoing performance or to respond to future changes to the business. Assuming the report is accurate, many decisions can be made based on the information presented in the financial statement. Also, the purpose the financial statement is to provide a proactive tool to:

- Understand the past and
- Understand the trends and cycles that are likely to occur based upon past and present results.

A review of the financial statement allows the financial manager to be proactive on financial matters for the future.

Understanding the Practicality

From a practical standpoint, the experienced practice administrator or manager is well-qualified to sift through the financial statement for issues of real importance. Through common sense, the wise manager can distinguish between areas of monetary importance and those with relative insignificance, correctly interpret and appropriately respond to valid problems, and not overact to minor issues.

Medical practice administrators should also be familiar with owner-important issues, known "hot buttons" (whether justified or not), and the proper response to issues. Conversely, if what is important is insignificant in the broader view, the administrator should help the physician-owner to accept the irrelevance of the concerns and move on.

Understanding the Effect

Financial statements help to identify future trends, adjust future operating results, and rectify past mistakes or flaws through improved future operational initiatives. With tactful and constructive observations, the administrator can address oversights to achieve greater fiscal responsibility in the months and years ahead.

The value of considering past omissions and lapses is to learn from the mistakes and to respond to the consequences in the future. For example, further review is warranted if the financial statements for a series of months reflect higher-than-budgeted personnel costs. Upon further analysis, if the discovery reveals that the excessive personnel costs are due to unauthorized overtime, then the manager can consider procedural and/or disciplinary action. The salient initiative in this example is not to criticize management for this oversight, but to correct the lapses and move forward.

Table 1-1 illustrates an example of an income statement. It contains actual entries to illustrate the basic financial information of a medical practice. Although simple financial statements usually depict operating performance in adequate detail, a more detailed breakdown of revenue and expenses tells the story behind the numbers. In Table 1-1, the income statement illustrates revenue and expenses before physician compensation. In most physician-owned practices, income is not guaranteed. Physician compensation (at least for the owners) is the practice's *profit*. In effect, as in any business, all excess earnings that remain after realizing expenses and overhead are the owner's profit or compensation.

REPORTING PRACTICE OPERATING RESULTS

To provide adequate information for management decisions, the reporting process must be timely, accurate, simple, sufficiently detailed, quantitative, and historical.

- **Timely.** Reflect recent historical results in reports.
- **Accurate.** Compile reliable and accurate data.
- **Simple.** Provide information that is easy to interpret and understand. Rather than submitting reams of computer paper and various spreadsheets of statistical data, reports should be simple and to the point.
- **Sufficiently detailed.** While trying to keep the report simple, sufficient detail (only on relevant matters) should be included for future decision-making. The overriding premise is to be proactive more than reactive.
- **Quantitative.** Use comparative analytical data from budgeted and prior-period actual performance totals as a benchmark for measuring current operating performance.
- **Historical data.** Use historical data primarily as the basis for making future decisions.

The reporting cycle should be completed on a regular basis—preferably monthly, but at least quarterly. Management will benefit by seeing operational results regularly, at the same time each month. Those responsible for submitting the financial results should complete the closeout of the prior period under consideration in a timely manner. A significant part of an efficient and effective financial analysis is providing management with the tools to make decisions. An effective financial analysis of the financial statement of a reporting period should:

- Include interpretation of the data, conclusions about the reporting period, and assessment of trends, summarized in a simple, concise statement that interprets and summarizes the data.

TABLE 1-1

Sample Income Statement

	Current Month			Year-to-Date		
	Budget	**Actual**	**% Variance**	**Budget**	**Actual**	**% Variance**
Income						
Charges						
Other Adjustments						
Other Receipts						
Total Income						
Expenses						
Salaries: Office						
Answering Service and Pager						
Automobile						
Consultant Fees						
Conventions and Meetings						
Contributions						
Depreciation						
Dues/Subscriptions						
Employee Benefits						
Gifts/Flowers						
Insurance (business)						
Insurance (malpractice)						
Laundry (uniforms)						
Legal and Accounting						
Medical Pamphlets and Books						
Miscellaneous						
Office Supplies and Expenses						
Postage						
Profit Sharing						
Rent						
Repairs and Maintenance						
Supplies (medical)						
Taxes and Licenses						
Telephone						
Transcription Fees						
X-ray Expense						
Total Expenses						
Operating Income <Loss>						

- Be objective, giving a true picture of the financial status of the practice.
- Consider positive and negative aspects of the financial information.

■ Be used to make informed decisions regarding the operations of the medical practice in the best interest of the physician-owners and their employees, for both near- and long-term results.

The ability to make sound business decisions increases when the information process includes precise, summarized reports with both written and verbal objective conclusions, and when there is ongoing consultation between management and the physician-owners.

FINANCIAL ANALYSIS SIMPLIFIED

Medical practice management has become more complex in recent years. The need for highly proficient and competent business specialists, such as degreed accountants and masters in business administration, has increased in medical practices, with such positions becoming the norm in larger practices. Although physician-owners are enhancing their skills in financial analysis, their lack of training (and time to invest) in this area calls for simplified financial analysis. Complicated computer-generated and spreadsheet-generated financial information can be overwhelming and serve no purpose. Chapter 8 provides examples of simple financial reports that use visual tools to interpret performance. Simplified methods of financial analysis, presented precisely and sometimes using visuals (not just numbers), generate better business decisions and engender a productive environment.

What Is Financial Analysis?

Financial analysis is the interpretation and evaluation of numerical relationships among components in financial reports. This transcends to action-oriented initiatives that may result in significant operational and structural changes that are needed to achieve improvements. For a medical practice, the most important financial report is its income statement (see Table 1-1). To a lesser extent, a balance sheet is a key financial report. Even in smaller practices that operate on a cash basis of accounting, a financial analysis can take on more than just these basic issues. For example, in cash-based accounting, accounts receivable, accounts payable, and certain accruals should be considered. These matters will be presented in greater detail in subsequent chapters.

Financial analysis entails identification of the relationship between income cost and cash flow. Decision makers, both management and physician-owners, can evaluate the financial health, leverage, and deployment of assets and determine the working capital of the practice.

Financial Analysis Perspectives

Management uses financial analysis for many purposes. Depending upon financial analysis perspectives, key principles should include:

■ **Operational control.** A system for ensuring that actions are carried out according to plan or for safeguarding assets.

- **Pricing/fee structure.** The quantity of one good or service, usually cash, asked in return for a unit of another good or service.

- **Cost evaluation.** The process of calculating the cost of activities, products, or services.

- **Procurement of capital (financing and/or investors).** Obtaining resources from (1) owners, and providing them with a return on their investment, and (2) creditors, and repaying amounts borrowed (or otherwise settling the obligation). In some instances, a lender may also have the right to be an owner-investor.

- **Major incremental performance (eg, departments within the practice).** Description of the changes in cost, expense, investment, cash flow, revenue, profit, and the like, if one or more units are produced or sold or if an activity is undertaken.

- **Department accountability.** Considering the various units of a medical practice as separate entities or profit centers, and giving the management of each unit the responsibility for their unit's revenues and expenses.

- **Profitability analysis.** An analysis of the net income within the entire organization and/or division, with respect to various comparatives, including the profit plan or budget, prior period(s), industry benchmarks, and internalized expectations (of the owners).

- **Return on capital analysis.** An analysis of income (before distributions to suppliers of capital) for a period. As a rate, this amount can be divided by the average total assets to derive a return on capital percent. Interest, net of tax effects, should be added back to net income for the numerator.

Traditionally, medical practices have not incorporated these fundamental principles into their management process. However, this process is essential to effective management in the future, whether practices are enlarging, maintaining, or downsizing.

Regardless of the analyst's point of view, financial viability must be interpreted in the following areas:

- Financial health of the practice
- Earning potential of the practice
- Liquidity of assets
- Assignment of risk

Each of these areas is critical in various forums, including: (1) to the existing owners of the practice, (2) as consideration for selling or merging the practice with another, and (3) to prospective new owners who are reviewing the viability of the practice as a future investment.

Financial Analysis Procedures

The three key areas of financial analysis procedures are as follows:

1. **Percentage statement analysis.** A statement containing, in addition to (or instead of) dollar amounts, the ratios of dollar amounts to some base. In a percentage income statement, the

base is usually either net revenue (after contractual allowances have been deducted from gross revenue) or net collections, if on a cash basis. The relationship of each major expense line as a percentage of revenue should be included on the income statement. This percentage should be compared against prior periods, industry benchmarks, and other viable comparisons. Sometimes, percentages will better illustrate operating performance than absolute dollars. For example, a practice with a 50% overhead rate should indicate how well the practice is functioning. Conversely, a specific dollar amount of overhead (relative to the 50%) would not necessarily provide much information about the practice's expense structure until or unless a complete review of the results of the entire statement is obtained.

2. **Ratios.** These represent the determination of financial statement entry relationships (ie, income statement item to income statement item, income statement item to balance sheet item). The resulting fractional structure provides quick, yet insightful references to performance. Ratios are generally used to assess aspects of profitability, solvency, and liquidity. Ratios are relationships between one key number and another, between income statement items and balance sheet items. Commonly used financial ratios are of three kinds: (a) those that summarize some aspect of operations for a period, usually a year; (b) those that summarize some aspect of financial position at a given moment — the moment for which a balance sheet has been prepared; and (c) those that relate some aspect of operations to some aspect of financial position. (See Chapter 5 for a detailed discussion of the types of ratios and their application.) Ratios are telltale in that they concisely present operating performance in certain key areas. They provide succinct summaries of performance and are often visually illustrated through charts and graphs.

3. **Variance analysis.** Such an analysis is the investigation of the causes of variances of both revenue and expenses. Every income statement should have an accompanying variance analysis summary report, which simply proactively describes those revenue and/or expense line items that are significantly over or under the benchmark or other comparative information. That comparison could be the prior period, the prior month, the budget, an industry benchmark, all of these, or a combination of all of these. A variance analysis can be a vitally important tool to supply to the physician owner of the practice. A variance analysis explicitly outlines variances between line items and brings them to the forefront of attention.

Actual financial analysis procedures are discussed in greater detail in subsequent chapters.

SUMMARY

In summary, understanding financial statements, other related
reports, and the subsequent reporting process is fundamental to the
successful financial management of the medical practice. Once these
basic standards are established, maintained, and adhered to month
after month, the foundation for a successful financial interpretation
and optimum management of the business will be in place. These
fundamentals should be primarily considered when addressing
more specific areas of financial management and understanding in
the medical practice. Accurate financial information provides the
administrator of the medical practice with the tools to complete a
precise analysis. Precise analysis increases the likelihood of
beneficial decisions and a successful business.

The Revenue Cycle

If a medical practice wishes to maximize its revenue, it should adhere to the fundamentals of business. Those fundamentals involve the determination and continued assurance that every component of the business that has anything to do with the generation or production of revenue (either directly or indirectly) is being effectively accomplished. For the medical practice, the end result of the patient encounter is the generation of revenue. The steps to revenue generation are similar to the progressive steps along an assembly line in a factory. In a medical practice, this assembly line is the revenue cycle of performance.

This chapter explores the various components that comprise the revenue cycle, along with other key indicators that contribute to maximization of revenue. In the medical practice, production of revenue starts with various processes that take place even prior to the patient encounter. Ultimately, they culminate with nonpatient encounter activities, including account billing, collection, and follow-up. To ensure that the income earned in the medical practice is, in fact, maximized, an effective progression through the revenue cycle is a must.

COMPONENTS OF THE REVENUE CYCLE

The purpose of this book is not to analyze the operational details pertaining to the revenue cycle (eg, appointment scheduling, registration, coding, charge capture, patient and insurance billing, account follow-up and collections, various other components of the revenue cycle). This chapter, however, briefly discusses these factors in the context of how they affect revenue.

Appointment Scheduling

Generally, revenue generation starts with the patient's call to schedule an appointment. Appointment scheduling can be a function of one department or one of many functions in a medical practice, largely dependent upon the size of the practice. Small practices rarely have the luxury of assigning one function to a department. They often have to rely on the participation of many staff members to handle this responsibility. For example, appointment scheduling is the receptionist's primary responsibility, but that position requires coverage from other employees, even clinical staff, during certain periods of the day when call-in volume is high.

The rudiments of appointment scheduling are to see the most patients within a given workday or workweek to maximize practice revenue. Revenue suffers when breakdowns in scheduling occur. This can happen when staff members do not understand the financial requirements of the practice and suit their own preferences rather than considering financial practicality. One example might be when the scheduler discourages late-day appointments so that everyone can leave at 5:00 p.m.—including the physician. Another example is when the scheduler fails to see the importance of accommodating walk-in patients or the significance of scheduling with the anticipation of a certain number of no-shows. Savvy scheduling techniques, such as filling predictably light days with well visits, physicals, and rechecks, and saving busy days for sick visits, can be monumental in attaining the revenue goals of the practice. (Not every practice focuses on volume; some financial systems are based on types of patients and cases. The important issue here is to have a scheduling policy that reflects the business model of the practice and the specialty and preferences of the physicians.)

Truthfully, physicians cannot generate revenue if they do not see patients, and revenue cannot be maximized without a steady stream of patients. Therefore, a healthy revenue cycle relies on proficient appointment scheduling.

Registration

Establishing a registration procedure to attain accurate patient information is an essential function of the revenue cycle, especially in the case of payments by third-party payers where accurate information equals reimbursement. (While Chapter 3 discusses expense controls in the context of the value of time versus quality, this issue is pertinent to the registration process.) In the instance of registration, the demographic (ie, name, address, telephone numbers, work place, and insurance coverage) information must be updated every time the patient sees the provider. When a breakdown of information gathering occurs, the registration process significantly impedes the practice's ability to maximize revenue.

The registration process in some instances is the patient's initial impression of customer service and patient care. Recognizing that registration is one part of the revenue cycle, the registrar should be pleasant, professional, and persistent in attaining complete and accurate demographic information from the patient.

Coding

Coding and proper documentation, a necessity to assure that revenue is appropriately recognized, starts with the education of the physician and staff. It also entails regular review of the coding procedures within the practice. Using a two-fold approach, coding reviews should be completed (1) internally, and (2) externally by a third party on a periodic basis to assess compliance. The primary purpose of most chart reviews is to assure compliance with Medicare and other guidelines. An additional benefit is the legitimate recognition of revenue through enhanced documentation or precise coding practices.

Another aspect of coding reviews can be the completion of a revenue analysis among the various providers within the practice to ascertain trends in coding and documentation. In a practice, physicians often see essentially the same type patients, but may document these encounters differently via diagnostic coding procedures. For example, Physician A might code most encounters at the Evaluation and Management Level Codes 3, 4, and 5, while Physician B may code the same procedures at Levels 2 and 3. By coding at a higher level, Physician A will generate greater revenue for the practice.

By conducting a periodic coding review, physicians can be continuously current on the changes that occur in coding. The practice should also make every effort to obtain reasonable, legitimate reimbursements from third-party payers for services rendered.

Charge Capture

Assuming the coding and documentation is accurate and effective, the revenue cycle moves from the clinical to the business side (ie, charge capture). Charge capture encompasses the appropriate transfer of the documentation and coding to the actual billing instrument. It is essential to capture all revenue for services that are legitimately performed. Sometimes a breakdown in the charge capture process is due to an ineffective superbill (ie, encounter form). The physician may have done the work and documented it appropriately, but if the encounter form is faulty—too confusing to complete or filled out improperly—the charge capture progression is interrupted. Encounter forms can be improved with continual review and communication between the physician and the support staff. In order to maximize revenue, staff members, who are responsible for accurate charge capture, must attain clarification from the physician when questions arise.

Patient and Insurance Billing

After the clinicians have done their part in proper coding and documentation of services, the business staff must ensure that the charge captures are accurate. The business office can then assume responsibility for accurate billing to patients and third-party insurers. Certainly in today's medical practice, the work of the insurance billing process must be done with total effectiveness. This entails using an appropriate practice management system, processing bills electronically, maintaining acceptable relations with the payers, devising internal information system processes, and creating other organizational steps. It is not the purpose of this book to review the efficiency of the aforementioned processes; however, in the context of the revenue cycle, it is a major component.

Training and implementation of billing policies and procedures are other major issues in the billing process. For maximum productivity, an effective billing office requires adequate organization, supervision, and oversight, and should offer incentives for collection performance. The physician and clinical staff can work hard to maximize patient encounters through proper coding and other functions, but all efforts are for naught without an effective billing office. If ineffective billing continues, the revenue cycle will break down, money will be lost, and the practice will not reach its maximum revenue potential.

Account Follow-up and Collections

The final component in the completion of the revenue cycle is account follow-up and collections. Numerous problems arise in the process of obtaining payment from the patient and third-party insurers, either as a result of mistakes made during the billing process or from slow payers who either refuse or cannot pay in a timely manner due to their own cash flow problems.

Constant follow-up on past due accounts is required in order to realize maximum revenue. Past due accounts should be monitored daily and specific accounts should be assigned to billing staff for follow-up. Simple past due notices seldom correct the problem with delinquent accounts. Practice personnel should persistently use telephone, email, and other means of communication to collect past due payments. Larger practices should organize a special collection department. Financial and other incentives can be used to motivate staffers who are charged with the difficult, challenging, and sometimes unpleasant task of collections.

Other Components of the Revenue Cycle

Major components of the revenue cycle have been outlined in the previous sections; however, within each of these areas there are other important components. They may not be a specific departmental function, but they are central to the efficiency of the revenue cycle and the practice's ability to maximize revenue. These components include the following:

- Patient refunds and credit balances
- Collection agency performance
- Fee schedule and pricing for medical services
- Staff education of policies and procedures, as well as compliance
- Timing of charge entry
- Claim denial and rejection trends and reasons
- Staff productivity goals

Each of these components is important and can result in revenue loss if the system breaks down. Issuing refunds is a time-consuming chore that is usually a result of miscalculations on the part of someone within the practice. Internal reviews should transpire to determine where problems have occurred to limit these refunds.

As a last resort, most practices use outside agencies for the collection of bad debts. However, by the time an account is turned over to a collection agency, profit is depleted and the practice is merely trying to recoup its cost (or at least a portion) to deliver the service.

The pricing of medical services is also important. Some insurers will pay closer to fee schedule than one might realize. For example, indemnity insurance, although less prominent in the marketplace, will often pay a reasonable customary charge for services rendered.

Education is essential to the efficient operation of the medical practice in order to ensure that the revenue cycle is maintained. Both staff and providers must receive regularly scheduled training in each area of the revenue cycle, through a combination of in-house training and by attending outside workshops and seminars.

Charge entry should be immediate, as revenue cannot be realized in cash until the charge is entered and the billing process starts. It is important to assure that the practice is collecting all co-pays and deductibles when services are rendered, both as a requirement of the managed care payer (plus Medicare/Medicaid) and as a good business practice.

Claim denial and rejection trends are major problems within many medical practices. They interrupt the revenue cycle, at least temporarily, and cause tremendous strain on the practice through additional work. The source of claim denials should be continuously investigated. The billing manager and claims administrator should regularly determine the reasons and source of those rejections, setting goals to reduce occurrences. Employee incentives can be established to help reach these goals and to keep rejections to a minimum.

Staff productivity is another major component of revenue maximization within the practice. Whether in the front or back office, or within the providers themselves, it is important to measure and evaluate productivity to ensure a successful practice.

KEY REVENUE INDICES

Figure 2-1 outlines key revenue indices by summary form key. Collections top the list within most medical practices (as with all businesses). Medical practices must develop a strategy for maximizing charges and get the most out of reimbursement in order to realize the highest collections. The components of charges include key areas of volumes (presumably generated by the providers), charge entry, fees, coding practices, and contract negotiations. Under reimbursements, payer mix, adjustments, denials, follow-up, front-end processes, payment posting, claims process, and contract management all relate to success in payments. These indices also form components of the revenue cycle that ultimately result in the realization of revenue for the practice.

FIGURE 2-1
Key Revenue Indices

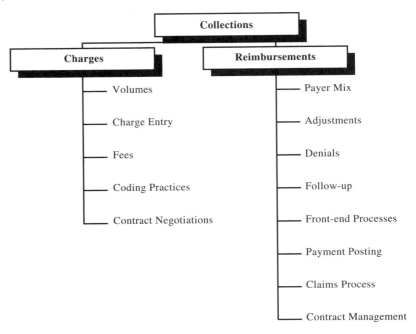

STEPS TO ASSURE REVENUE MAXIMIZATION

The following six steps can be used to assure revenue maximization in the medical practice. Some of these steps relate to the previous discussions concerning the revenue cycle and are important reminders for the practice.

Step 1: Analyze the Practice's Revenue Cycle

The revenue cycle begins when a patient schedules an appointment and ends when the practice receives payment for services rendered. All steps in between should be appropriately conducted and verification of key revenue indices (Figure 2-1) should be efficiently completed.

Step 2: Document Financial Policies and Procedures

Written financial policies and procedures are essential to assure that the practice is appropriately recording and realizing its revenue and to maintain consistency in all areas of practice operations. Personnel turnover, an expected event in most practices, can cause a breakdown in the revenue cycle unless policies and procedures for carrying out certain functions are thoroughly documented. Particularly in the beginning, the replacement of the person at the receptionist desk increases the likelihood of certain procedures being left undone, especially if the new employee does not understand the practice's policies and procedures and has no written documentation to rely upon for reference. Through lack of knowledge, the new receptionist may fail to collect co-pays and deductibles, for example, causing a drain on the practice's revenue generation.

Practices without well-documented policies and procedures within each major department and billing policies and procedures are apt to realize less revenue and to be less successful. However, having policies in place does not assure that the guidelines will be followed. The practice administrator must be sure that employees read, understand, and follow the prescribed policies and procedures with recourse for noncompliance. Consistency is essential. Few, if any, exceptions should be permitted with respect to following established policies and procedures.

Step 3: Review the Financial Tools

A properly used superbill or encounter form will reduce claims processing time and provide for appropriate and fair payment. In order for the form to be effective, it must be user-friendly and easy for the provider to code.

Constant review of all the financial tools, such as the superbill, encounter form, and other documentation that lead to the charge entry, should regularly occur to prevent a breakdown in efficiency and to safeguard against increases in lost revenue.

Step 4: Review Managed Care Contracts

Every managed care contract should have a contractual obligation that requires payment within specific, pre-established time frames. Fee schedules and other requirements should be presented in the contract. The providers in the practice should also understand the contract requirements, which typically include preauthorization and precertification. Contract policies should be outlined and documentation should be available for staff to follow. Otherwise, the potential increases for denied claims. The provider should not perform services where the contract will not provide reimbursement. Thus, the managed care process should be a major component within the practice's business management strategy. Normally, in a small practice, the administrator is responsible for contract management, but larger practices may designate one employee to oversee the managed care/reimbursement processes.

All such contracts should be bilateral. They call for negotiation, either directly or indirectly, through an affiliation such as an independent practice association or a physician hospital organization. The capacity for acceptable reimbursement within a medical practice is largely based upon the sophistication of interpretation and the understanding of the managed care contracts.

Step 5: Review the Practice's Current Fee Schedule

It is essential to compare the fee schedule to certain standards, including benchmarks or history of reimbursement within the practice, at least once a year to ensure that all the codes are updated and fees are set at reasonable levels. Sometimes, an increase in the fees will only increase the contractual adjustments, not providing additional net revenue to the practice. This proves to be of little value if not actually realized through reimbursement. Conversely, if some increased payments result, it is quite beneficial.

Step 6: Make Sure the Practice Is Compliant

Compliance with regulatory rules, which requires significant effort, is a major factor for medical practices. The advantage to regulatory compliance is that physicians and employees are provided the education that often serves to enhance the production of revenue.

REVENUE ENHANCEMENT

In addition to the aforementioned enhancement steps, there are other specific areas where the practice can increase revenue. One step involves reviewing productivity by individual physician, code, encounter, and visit. Others steps include specific initiatives, such as opening new sites, adding providers, expanding access, and adding new services, all of which contribute to the overall effort and result in enhanced productivity and revenue.

SOURCES OF REVENUE

The revenue assessment (ie, tracking the sources of revenue within the practice) enables the practice administrator and the physician to identify the most profitable areas of revenue production and to discover the cause of lost revenue.

Within every medical practice, revenue may be tied to specific production and revenue centers. Common revenue sources include:

- Patient encounters or visits within the outpatient practice
- Surgical procedures
- Ancillary services, including laboratory, radiology, and other diagnostics
- Pharmacy
- Specific procedures, such as flexible sigmoidoscopy, bone densitometry, and so on

Determining the revenue generated within each center will provide information for financial planning and management. Revenue centers are easy to separate by type of service performed. When looking at sources of revenue, especially those that relate to managed care contracting, it is important to determine services that generate the greatest and most profitable levels of production. For example, an analysis of both the ability to produce revenue and the cost to produce it should identify the areas of production (ie, revenue) that require the greatest emphasis. It is possible to determine that the best and most profitable source of revenue for an internal medicine physician is certain in-office procedures, such as flexible sigmoidoscopies. In addition, there may be opportunities to add ancillary services that will at least offset some of the fixed overhead in the practice and allow the creation of volume that absorbs that overhead. However, a careful review may reveal that certain ancillary services that appear to offset overhead may do no more than reduce profit margins because the cost of supplying those services is greater than the revenue produced.

Cost accounting is an important concept in the management process in which several services/departments are provided. Each product or service should have a separate accounting with allocations of both revenue and cost. Cost accounting for a particular product or service in the practice is an especially appropriate way to evaluate performance and make decisions on whether to continue to offer these services in the future. Revenue is easily separated by profit center or service.

Expense allocation is more difficult because of unavoidable allocations from general corporate overhead (see Chapter 3). Certain expenses are more difficult than is revenue to relate directly to a particular service or product. It is important, nevertheless, to separate revenue by the type of service. An example of different components within a medical practice and how the revenue can be separated is illustrated in Table 2-1 and Table 2-2.

PRODUCTIVITY DEFINED

Productivity is measurable (or defined) in many ways within the medical practice. For example, consider the following productivity measures:

- Visits/encounters
- Office visits
- Procedures
- Consults
- Inpatient revenue
- Ancillary services
- Relative Value Units (RVUs)
- Charges
- Gross charges
- Net charges
- Collections
- Gross collections
- Net collections

When considering each of these measures in the context of a broad definition of productivity, visits and encounters may be gauged by the number of encounters and procedures. Inevitably, these encounters have to be transferred to revenue of some sort, as will other types of productivity measures, including RVUs, charges, and collections.

Using RVUs as a standard is increasing in acceptance throughout the health care industry. Essentially, RVUs are a measure of productivity based upon the Medicare established Resource Based

T A B L E   2-1

Physician	OV	Consultation	Hospital	Radiology	Lab	Echo/U/s	Skin/Flex Venipuncture	Resp/Join Insurance	Immun
A	$187,250	$399	$3,940	$25,239	$67,780	$10,529	$5,281	$18,787	$2,465
B	$138,136	$91	$2,553	$11,442	$42,482	$2,830	$10,238	$10,022	$2,107
C	$171,734		$18,031	$29,496	$43,030	$12,471	$7,100	$18,021	$4,765
D	$166,204	$160	$7,121	$46,392	$62,579	$12,602	$4,541	$14,168	$5,661
E	$240,887	$1,003	$13,145	$42,363	$46,119	$29,049	$12,687	$25,714	$18,889
F	$123,224			$6,127	$16,777		$6,392	$6,206	$2,421
G	$193,508	$2,434	$10,253	$39,241	$39,242	$14,358	$9,252	$18,642	$3,347
H	$161,722	$989	$18,865	$30,582	$35,432	$14,024	$10,017	$16,236	$7,639
I	$177,497	$315	$6,810	$12,308	$20,793	$9,142	$1,917	$4,508	$4,430
J	$198,503		$5,765	$1,367	$35,028	$13,088	$7,975	$4,173	$3,139
K	$49,257	$1,152	$2,845	$6,418	$561	$1,089	$1,683	$354	$1,231
L	$97,730			$314	$8,551	$863	$4,777	$3,997	
Total	**$1,924,128**	**$5,391**	**$87,916**	**$263,777**	**$428,659**	**$120,804**	**$82,471**	**$143,095**	**$57,356**

Source: The Coker Group © 2002.

T A B L E   2-2

Physician	OV	Consultation	Hospital	Radiology	Lab	Echo/U/s	Skin/Flex Venipuncture	Resp/Join Insurance	Immun
A	58.21%	0.12%	1.22%	7.85%	21.07%	3.27%	1.64%	5.84%	0.77%
B	62.82%	0.04%	1.16%	5.20%	19.32%	1.29%	4.66%	4.56%	0.96%
C	56.37%	0.00%	5.92%	9.68%	14.12%	4.09%	2.33%	5.92%	1.56%
D	52.03%	0.05%	2.23%	14.52%	19.59%	3.95%	1.42%	4.44%	1.77%
E	56.04%	0.23%	3.06%	9.86%	10.73%	6.76%	2.95%	5.98%	4.39%
F	76.47%	0.00%	0.00%	3.80%	10.41%	0.00%	3.97%	3.85%	1.50%
G	58.59%	0.74%	3.10%	11.88%	11.88%	4.35%	2.80%	5.64%	1.01%
H	54.73%	0.33%	6.38%	10.35%	11.99%	4.75%	3.39%	5.49%	2.59%
I	74.67%	0.13%	2.86%	5.18%	8.75%	3.85%	0.81%	1.90%	1.86%
J	73.78%	0.00%	2.14%	0.51%	13.02%	4.86%	2.96%	1.55%	1.17%
K	77.74%	0.00%	1.82%	4.49%	10.13%	0.89%	1.72%	2.66%	0.56%
L	83.20%	0.00%	0.00%	0.27%	7.28%	0.73%	4.07%	3.40%	1.05%
Total	**61.80%**	**0.17%**	**2.82%**	**8.47%**	**13.77%**	**3.88%**	**2.65%**	**4.60%**	**1.84%**

Source: The Coker Group © 2002.

Relative Value System (RBRVS). Within that system, the Center for Medicare and Medicaid Services (CMS) annually establishes a standard for most Current Procedural Terminology (CPT) codes. Most codes carry an RVU value. The RVUs consist of three components: work or professional component, practice expense, and malpractice cost. Typically, the work or professional component includes the physician's resource time, skill, stress, physical status of care delivery, and judgment involved within each procedure. The practice expense includes the operating cost and, perhaps accurately phrased, the general overhead. The malpractice component is the professional liability expense.

RVUs are simply the measured operating standard for gauging productivity. It can be an effective measuring tool because it is based on an independent standard that is established by CMS and adjusted annually with varying values per CPT code. RVUs serve as the conduit for leveling the playing field. A value of each service relative to another helps to measure productivity regardless of the actual reimbursement processes.

The advantage of the RVU system is that it eliminates the disparities in reimbursement for similar services from one third-party payer to another. The disadvantage is that RVUs are not revenue; in reality, RVUs are not relevant to what is actually occurring. Therefore, in terms of real reimbursement, measuring productivity by RVUs should be considered with balance. They can be useful internally to determine how one physician or provider is performing relative to another, given the legitimate differences in reimbursement that may exist. RVUs, however, are not appropriate when practices need to be evaluated for their total performance from the standpoint of true financial analysis.

Gross charges and net charges are also very valid measurements of productivity. Gross charges, which can be considered the *full fee schedule* charges, are typically all charges generated by the practice, regardless of actual reimbursement or before discounting. Although gross charges are a valid method used to determine productivity within a practice from one provider to another, they have little reality as to bottom-line performance. A practice should be careful using gross charges as a measurement or standard of productivity because they do not truly reflect the revenue collected by the practice. In comparison to the retail industry, gross charges are amounts brought in prior to markdowns or discounts. Gross charges are valid measurements of productivity, but do not reflect actual performance.

Net charges, however, reflect what the practice expects to collect after all markdowns or discounts are taken. Net charges reflect the true performance expectations of the medical practice after consideration of all discounts; they are probably the most valid representation of productivity.

Gross and net collections reflect what is actually being brought into the practice. In many instances, cash versus accrual basis of accounting will differentiate between gross and net collections and gross and net charges. Gross collections are those collections brought in for all professional services before any refunds or credits. Net collections are those collections that are realized after all refunds are considered. Depending upon the context of the review, net charges and collections would be the most valid measurements of productivity, primarily because they reflect real world results.

SUMMARY

Management of the revenue cycle is an enormous responsibility for any practice, especially the owner and administrator. Methods, measurement, recording, and consideration of any component of the revenue cycle require management's day-to-day awareness to attain maximum revenue. Medical practices cannot afford to lose a single dollar of legitimate revenue that is due. Without constant attention to each aspect of the revenue cycle, losses will likely occur.

chapter 3

Controlling Expenses

Medical practice expenses actually encompass many aspects, including basic control of all outgoing disbursements of the practice and, in its strictest sense, operating expenses and disbursements to physicians and other providers, even if they are owners of the business.

This chapter primarily focuses on the expenses prior to physician compensation. In most private medical practices, physician compensation is merely the *operating profit* that remains after all overhead has been paid. Although some employed providers are part of the *overhead*, the most accurate way to consider the expense structure of the practice is prior to any physician or provider payments, including salary and benefits. The objective of this chapter is to consider the best ways to control general operational expenses (ie, overhead).

EXPENSE MANAGEMENT

A slightly different way of approaching general operational expenses is through expense management, which requires:

- Knowledge of how overhead expenses will be presented, reviewed, and analyzed
- Comprehension of some of the basic concepts (ie, definitions) of expenses
- Attention to specific areas that comprise the majority of a practice's expenditures

Comparisons of Expenses on the Income Statement

There are three possible ways to present and compare expenses on the profit and loss statement: (1) comparison to budget, (2) comparison to prior period, and (3) comparison to benchmarks. Comparing expenses to budget, if done with thought and careful analysis, is the preferred basis. Budget and pro formas must follow a defined plan with numbers formulated on a viable basis. (See Chapter 7 for more information on budgeting and pro formas.)

Accuracy is essential in budgeting. A budget is a plan for revenue and expenses. It is not the actual performance totals. The more accurate the budget, the more useful it will be as a management tool.

In comparing actual performance to budgets, the budget is considered the *profit plan*. The profit plan connotes a proactive process and a more relevant total upon which to compare actual performance. The budget (or profit plan) considers what is the most current depiction of the practice's operations, assuming it is based upon present operational expenses and is most reflective of the daily number of providers, locations, and so on.

It may also be worthwhile to compare expenses to the prior period, defined as the prior month or the same month in the prior year, and year-to-date totals for both. This comparison can be of some value if the comparative totals are relevant. For example, if the practice has increased or decreased its number of providers in the two periods, the comparison will be irrelevant. It is important to assure that the numbers are relevant, or they can be easily misconstrued.

Benchmarks are also a valid way to compare expenses, yet they should be realistically reviewed. Benchmarks are often abused when used as the only standard. Expenses should be controlled, based on the history and knowledge of how the practice should operate. Benchmarks (discussed in detail in Chapter 5) should be carefully used when comparing expenses.

COMMON SIZING

Common sizing is when expenses are stated as a percentage of gross or net revenue or net collections, depending upon the basis of accounting being used. This allows for quick identification of performance and compares such actions with differences that are relative to productivity. On an accrual basis, expenses are compared to net revenue or net charges in the process. On a cash basis, expenses are compared to net collections. Common sizing speaks in terms of percentages rather than absolute dollars. It provides an insight into the practice's operations. Practice overhead may be considered relative to a total pie that includes the revenue. The portion of that pie that is not concerned with operating overhead is left for the physician-owners, via compensation and benefits. Preferably, the pie shows no more than 60% expenses, leaving at least 40% for the physician-owners. This, in effect, is the process of common sizing. Profit and loss statements should provide a column that includes the expenses percentage to revenue (preferably net revenue or net collections), which furnishes an informative summary of practice expenses. Many of the benchmarks that are used will be presented in a common-sized manner.

VARIANCE ANALYSIS

Another key element used to accurately and realistically analyze expenses is the variance analysis. When other comparative totals are illustrated, including common sizing, statements must isolate those expenses that indicate significant variance from the comparative column. Whether the comparative is the budget, prior period, or benchmarks, any significant diversion from the plan or the comparative requires an explanation. This forces the analyzer of the expenses to focus on the most important areas where significant dollars have changed. The variance analysis may also be dependent upon significant changes in percentages. In the medical practice, if personnel expense has been budgeted for $20,000 per month, and the results have consistently been $25,000 per month, the effect is a 25% increase over the plan, as well as a $5,000 additional expense. The reason for this variance, both in percentages and in dollars, deserves an explanation. This information will help the physician-owner learn more about the financial management of the business and understand the causes of such variances. It forces the manager of the practice to research the reasons for significant changes in expenses. Explanations may also be in order when numbers are significantly under budget. Some of the discoveries may require certain management decisions; hence, the inherent benefit of the analysis.

These comparisons are useful tools for the manager who must understand and control expenses. Early warning signals detected through variance analysis, common sizing analysis, and comparisons to the budget or prior period benchmarks are all great management tools for controlling expenses. A trite, but true, statement is that if we don't know an expense is excessive, we cannot control it. The sooner the problem is discovered, the easier it will be to solve. Early warning signals are invaluable in controlling expenses in the practice over the course of a year. These analyses provide such early warning signals.

TYPES OF EXPENSES

There are four basic classifications of expenses:

- Fixed expenses that remain stable regardless of volume
- Variable expenses that vary with volume
- Semi-variable expenses that vary with ranges of volume
- Expenses that remain stable for a range of volume and then increase incrementally

It is essential to understand the characteristics of the four classifications, especially the two basic expenses—fixed and variable. Most expenses in the medical practice are fixed (or semi-fixed). They include such costs as rent, malpractice insurance, information systems, furniture/equipment (via depreciation, and personnel costs [to some extent]). Personnel expenses, however, can become semi-variable (or semi-fixed) expenses over time when, for example, additional staff is needed or overtime is worked. Because fixed expense is such a large portion of the total practice overhead (prior to realizing provider compensation and benefits), it is essential that this classification of expenses be controlled. The good news is that once a certain amount of fixed expense is absorbed, any additional revenue will be mostly profitable. However, the bad news is that fixed expenses will exist regardless of how much revenue is generated. Thus, in the low revenue-generating practice, the fixed expense will be a much greater percentage (common-sized), resulting in lower margins (incomes) to the physicians.

Variable expenses are less controllable, yet should only change with volume. Because they are a much smaller percent of the total overhead, they have less of an effect on total profitability. They are very important, nevertheless, as a part of the expense control process. Variable expenses include office, medical, and pharmaceutical supplies.

Figure 3-1 illustrates the relationship between fixed and variable expenses, and the results of profitability opportunities. This figure readily shows that fixed expenses encompass a certain segment of the total practice overhead, which is in effect plotted via a straight line. Variable expenses are plotted on an angled line, with the profitability being all that results over the plotted breakeven point. This shows the operating loss area, as well as the operating income area. Once fixed costs are covered, they will effectively remain unchanged even with increases in income. The only expense that results after fixed costs are covered is a small portion of variable expenses. Therefore, the profitability of the practice greatly increases at that point.

To translate the theory in Figure 3-1 into the real-world medical practice, the opportunities for increased income are usually stated in a practical way. For example, the most practical way to generate an increase in income is to simply increase the number of encounters per day (based upon the knowledge of the average amount of revenue per encounter). As a result, the number of encounters may be plotted on a similar graph to illustrate the breakeven point. Figure 3-2 shows that once fixed costs are covered, the practice can generate greater operating margins merely by changing the additional variable.

FIGURE 3-1

Cost-Volume-Profit Graph

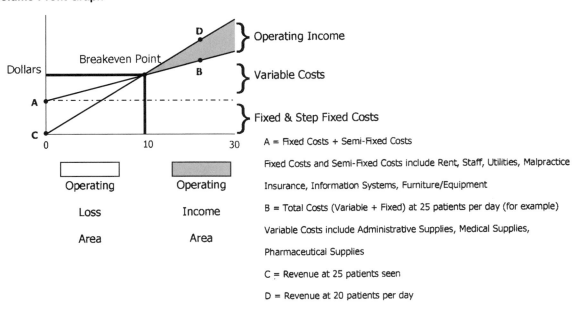

Source: Elizabeth W. Woodcock, Physicians Practice, Inc. Reproduced with permission.

FIGURE 3-2

Revenue per Encounter

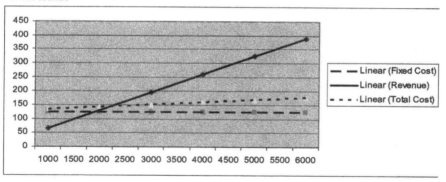

In thousands

In Figure 3-2, the vertical column of the graph is expensed in thousands of dollars of revenue. The horizontal line considers number of patient encounters. The illustration depicts how profit (the space between the revenue and expense lines) increases as the angular line of revenue goes up. The revenue increase can also be readily seen in Figure 3-2. For example, at 3,000 patient encounters per year, the practice will generate a revenue total of $200,000. The profitability is much lower at that point, probably $50,000. Compare those results to the performance results at 6,000 patient encounters. At that level, revenue is $400,000 and expenses are only about $175,000, so profit is $225,000. This clearly illustrates that with virtually the same amount of fixed costs between the two levels of productivity, the only difference is a small increase in variable expenses as the number of patient encounters/revenue increases. In this example, revenue is increased by 100 percent (eg, $400,000 versus $200,000) while expenses have only increased by $25,000 (variable expenses). This is the key to profitable operations in the medical practice (and most other businesses). Because a medical practice has mostly fixed expenses, increased revenue has a significant effect on the bottom line, perhaps more than in any other industry.

By way of review, fixed costs usually represent 70% to 80% of the expenses prior to provider compensation for most practices. Additional and marginal units of productivity disproportionately add to a practice's profitability. Fixed expenses are spread over more service units as productivity increases, which result in a reduction of per unit cost. The outcome is increased marginal income. This basic, important concept supports a simple, but essential, element of understanding for the physician: more patient encounters/procedures completed over a fixed period (ie, day, week, month, or year) equals greater profit and compensation.

DIRECT AND INDIRECT EXPENSES

Medical practices also have direct and indirect expenses. By definition, *direct expenses* can be traced to a specific medical service that is provided (eg, salary expense, supplies, materials used in providing the service). *Indirect expenses* are those that cannot be traced to a specific service (eg, rent, utilities, accounting). The importance of differentiating between direct and indirect expenses is the ability to control these expenses. Direct expenses are usually more controllable because they relate to income production. Indirect expenses sometimes are more complicated because they appear to be separated from the overall productivity of the practice. Even so, both are significant and essential.

Expenses, whether fixed, variable, direct, or indirect, may be broken down into five major classifications as follows:

- Staffing
- General and administrative (G&A)
- Facility strategies
- Medical/lab/radiology supplies
- Incentive strategies

Figure 3-3 illustrates the relationship of the major classifications of expenses to the total overhead of a typical practice. Staffing expenses (ie, salaries, benefits) are by far the greatest expenditure in the practice. Other expenses, while less than staffing expenses, are still quite significant. In considering these expenses in the following section, keep in mind the relationship between the total overhead of the practice (ie, all expenses prior to provider compensation and benefits).

Staffing

Staffing in the medical practice includes all employees other than the providers. A practice needs adequate staff to support the services that are performed. The number may vary largely from practice to practice, with some, based upon their design, history, and specialty, requiring more employees than others. Benchmarks are helpful for estimating staffing ratios, usually stated as number of full-time equivalent (FTE) employees in relation to providers. (See Chapter 5 for more information on ratios.)

FIGURE 3-3

Expenses and Overhead of a Typical Medical Practice

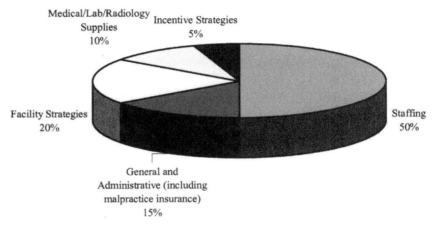

Providers are generally defined as any individual who is directly generating professional fees. Nonphysician providers may not carry a full 1.0 provider status in relationship to the physicians. Staffing numbers should be measured in the framework of each individual practice. One of the greatest challenges for most practices is to determine excess staffing capacity versus volume or productivity totals. In this case, common sizing of this expense is vital. For example, a medical practice that has a 25% to 30% personnel and benefit expense to net charges (or net collections) ratio is usually within the boundaries of reason. This will result in approximately 50% to 60% of the total overhead expense derived from personnel expense (assuming revenue is approximately double the practice overhead).

A key approach to managing personnel expenses is to consistently administer workflow through adequate cross training of staff and process review. Another consideration is the skill mix of the staff. In some instances, physicians will have a staffing preference, such as maintaining a long-standing employee, perhaps a registered nurse, whose salary is at a higher level. This may be a wise decision if the efficiency level is also higher, even though the direct cost may be greater.

Ideally, the medical practice staff should have a well-balanced skill set. A practice with highly trained and experienced staff is at an advantage over the practice that employs nonskilled and inexperienced workers. Take heed though, the cost of such a skill set may be prohibitive. To determine the right balance, one strategy might be to blend employees with different skills and experience levels. Through training and development, these employees will increase in their capacity to handle greater responsibilities within the practice.

Outsourcing of job functions is another alternative employment option. Typically, practices limit outsourcing to specific departments, such as billing and collections. Although outsourcing job functions usually entails a greater direct expense than the cost of employment, the increased efficiency may justify the arrangement. Every effort must be made to conduct ongoing analysis of the feasibility and proficiency of outsourcing. From a cost perspective, employment usually is the better alternative, unless trained and experienced staff are unavailable or the need of the outsourced resource is limited to an interim period.

The technology requirements for computerization and knowledge of practice management systems may limit the capacity for some practices to internally handle billing and collections. In some cases, billing operations are now being converted to application service providers (ASPs) with an Internet host arrangement. This arrangement cuts back on other areas of expense, including personnel staffing and computer systems.

Each practice should review its outsourcing alternatives and choose from available resources based on its unique circumstances. Some may opt to outsource virtually all of their personnel management functions to entities such as management service organizations (MSOs), or engage in employee leasing arrangements.

Although employee leasing arrangements are usually at a higher cost, they may also enhance efficiency; thus, they become a valid solution. As the single greatest expense in the practice, personnel management should receive a proportionate level of commitment and attention. Generally, this applies to the management of tasks and procedures. For example, the practice may be sufficiently staffed, yet employees may be required to work overtime due to poor patient flow, inefficient patient management, and inadequate provider productivity. In this case, overtime expenses will unnecessarily increase the personnel costs. Staffing expenses that exceed 50% of the total preprovider expense overhead (see Figure 3-3) calls for a detailed analysis of the cause. Stated differently, staffing expense greater than 30% of net revenue should also initiate a detailed analysis and review.

Staffing expenses should be reviewed daily in an effort to maintain control and to eliminate excessive costs. Controlling these expenses while maintaining high morale and attaining sufficient output from employees is the ultimate challenge in medical practice management.

Figure 3-4 summarizes major staffing strategies. These nine strategies, if followed, will improve practice operations, use the staff most efficiently, and control this significant expense.

General and Administrative Expenses

The practice should establish a reasonable percentage target for the general and administrative (G&A) category and monitor its performance. G&A expenses encompass a myriad of individual items, including catchalls such as:

- Accounting/legal contributions
- Dues and subscriptions (nonprovider)
- Malpractice insurance
- Janitorial
- Postage
- Maintenance and repairs
- Other professional services

G&A expenses are a broad classification that includes many important expenses. Individually, these expenses are not significant when compared to the total overhead (or percent of total net revenue), yet when combined, they comprise a significant portion of the overhead, perhaps as much as 15% to 20% of the pie (see Figure 3-3).

Most G&A expenses are costs associated with services provided (at least in part) by outside suppliers or professionals, such as for accounting and legal work and nonemployee-related insurance costs. Dues and subscriptions, maintenance and repair, and janitorial services are expenses provided by vendors outside of the medical practice. Continuous review of vendor invoices for accurate pricing of services and fulfillment is key to controlling G&A expenses. Many of these vendor organizations use a purchase order system to

FIGURE 3-4
Major Staffing Strategies

Strategy 1: Increase Volume
- Patient encounters
- Procedures
- Ancillary services

Strategy 2: Increase number of providers served per staff (FTE)
- Apply realism

Strategy 3: Review systems to identify inefficiencies
- Eliminate tasks/steps
- Minimize exceptions

Strategy 4: Evaluate staff skill mix
- Review credentials
- Evaluate skill sets

Strategy 5: Minimize turnover
- Identify critical performance measurements
- Hire staff with multi-task skills
- Cross train after employment
- Create stable environment
- Use predictably consistent management structure
- Reward performance
- Include incentive pay

Strategy 6: Remove incompetent staff
- Use legal and professional approach

Strategy 7: Provide adequate staff training
- Conduct regular training at all levels

Strategy 8: Ensure that personnel and compliance policies are written and followed
- Perform self-audit and periodic independent reviews

Strategy 9: Establish realistic salary ranges for practice positions
- Be competitive and consistent

---

authorize their services and they will assist the practice to help monitor and control expenses. Another method of controlling expenses is to designate one person as being responsible for purchasing and vendor selection. Ideally, with guidelines in place, the purchasing responsibility will be handled objectively in order to make the best decisions possible for the practice. Regardless of the method, every practice needs to have systems in place for oversight of expenses and guidelines for purchasing goods and services.

In all, G&A expenses are a significant factor in managing practice overhead. With systems and protocols in place, employers must monitor these expenses closely to ensure that practice funds are appropriately and cost-effectively used. Each component of G&A expense may appear to be relatively minor in comparison to the total expense pie; however, collectively, they comprise a significant amount and, therefore, warrant careful scrutiny and authorization.

Facility Strategies

Facility expenses relate to rent, utilities, and other direct expenses associated with the consumption of space. They are a major practice outlay. For the most part, medical practices will negotiate their leases on a fixed basis, which does not allow a great deal of flexibility given the fact that rent does not vary with volume. Therefore, the control of facility expense is accomplished by maximizing volume and revenue generation within the existing space, possibly by increasing the number of providers, utilizing the space more effectively, and increasing the hours of service. Another strategy is to sublet the space to other providers or entities, which in effect lowers the rental expense. A possible strategy to minimize expense might be to downsize the facility, sublet the space, and/or renegotiate to fewer square feet.

An added aspect of facility expense is the cost of utilities. By reducing the cost of utilities, facility expenses will ultimately decrease. Ways to control utilities include installing a system for monitoring the consumption of electricity, controlling the use of telephone expense (ie, long distance charges), and tracking other necessary, but most nonrevenue-producing commodities.

If the practice's facility expenses are at a particularly high percentage of the overhead, it may be possible to renegotiate the lease. If the rent is higher than the practice can afford, and as long as rates are based on the fair market value (ie, Stark, anti-kickback, other regulations or legal constraints), renegotiation of the lease is a reasonable strategy that should not be discounted.

The target is for the facility expense to be less than 10% of net revenue and 15% to 20% of the total overhead pie.

Medical/Lab/Radiology Supplies

Medical supplies vary greatly depending on the type of practice. Some practices consume and spend more on supplies, although, as a variable expense, the percentage to revenue should remain the same. Most practices do not spend a great deal on medical supplies relative to revenue, yet the expense is significant and should, thus, be closely monitored. Usually, medical supplies comprise 3% to 5% of net revenue and 6% to 10% of the total overhead pie.

The recommended way for obtaining quotes from major medical supply vendors is to use request for proposals (RFPs). Continuously using the same supplier may not be wise unless that vendor's prices are always justified. Over the course of time, it may be wise to consider other suppliers in an effort to keep prices down. It may also be appropriate to participate in a purchasing consortium. Finally, it is best to keep the inventory of medical supplies to a minimum. Easily being able to procure items justifies little need for maintaining a large inventory of supplies. The inventory is merely costing the practice more in storage space and money by tying up working capital for the excessive stock.

Incentive Strategies

The cost of incentives may not be considered a major expenditure within the medical practice, yet they are quite meaningful to the recipients. Incentive compensation moves employees to produce in the workplace and to adhere to their expected responsibilities and duties, which is essential. Employees can be awarded incentives in many ways, such as additional compensation, retirement plans, and special prizes and/or recognition. Incentive programs should be designed to generate the greatest response from the staff. In addition, staff should feel that they have an input in the process, not only for the incentives themselves, but also for ways to improve operations. Communication pipelines that allow employees to convey their suggestions and ideas are great ways to develop incentive programs. Compensation is of obvious high importance to most employees. Allowing employees to share in the practice's good operating results, improvements, cost savings, and other areas is a positive initiative. Longevity of service, which is important to any business' success, can be promoted through retirement and profit-sharing programs that are ultimately tied to the performance of the practice.

Figure 3-5 summarizes key ideas for stimulating morale and implementing incentives within the practice. By using incentives, the employer can attempt to control costs by influencing the employees to examine all expenses in an effort to maximize revenue for the practice.

F I G U R E 3-5

Employee Incentives

Strategy 1: Suggestion box
Strategy 2: Bright ideas program
Strategy 3: Profit-sharing/pension plans

FLOW SOURCE DOCUMENTS

In every instance, a practice needs to have certain policies and procedures in place for controlling expenses, including purchase orders, invoices, check requests, and contracts, where appropriate. Regardless of the transaction (eg, purchase of supplies, area of G&A expense, facility-related expense), systems should be established for the physician, or other individual who is in charge, to have the appropriate documents in place prior to authorizing payment or signing the check. With supporting documents in hand, the bills can be paid or questions can be asked for expenses that need further review. This will ensure the control of expenses, both internal and ongoing, from their source, at the time of payment.

VALUE-BASED EXPENSE MANAGEMENT

Key areas of expenses in the medical practice can be viewed from a value-based expense standpoint (ie, whether they add or take away value based upon the critical business processes as they are performed). The cost of any business process should also be considered based upon the time in which it takes to complete it, the quality of the work produced, and the actual dollars invested. Just because a process might require more time, does not necessarily mean that it is an unwarranted expense. Conversely, because more time is taken, there may be a lack of quality or additional expense due to the excessive amount of time taken to complete the process. Service that has value is usually done accurately without repetitive processes (ie, it is done right the first time). It also meets the customer's expectations, and as a result, the customer is more apt to pay for the service. Conversely, a nonvalue added service encompasses a greater cost to the supplier of that value. It often entails the need for correction or revision and in many cases requires an excessive review and waiting time. Such shortcomings lead to inefficiencies in the medical practice.

Various services can be measured in this manner (ie, value added versus nonvalue added). One example is the reception area, which is of major importance for any medical practice and normally the point of first contact (other than by telephone) between the patient and practice personnel. The receptionist's role includes a variety of functions that call for efficiency and customer friendliness on behalf of the practice. The receptionist must be pleasant, welcome the patient, acquire demographic information and other insurance data, and have a chart ready for the rest of the practice to use. In some instances, the reception area will also be responsible for collecting payments at the time of service.

If the reception area/function is considered in terms of quality and time management, it has a significant effect upon the practice's overall expense structure. For example, if the chart is not retrieved and ready, other members of the practice staff will spend time locating it. If demographic and insurance information is not updated at each visit, additional, unnecessary work will be required later. The additional time requirements are nonvalue added.

The practice should consider various functions in relevance to the amount of time required within the practice. Figure 3-6 illustrates a typical patient encounter in terms of time. In Figure 3-7, the same encounter is displayed in terms of a possible cost to the practice. It is easy to see that such cost is magnified when additional time is taken to complete the encounter. Most importantly, this is critical when the physician's time is exceeded above that which is normal. Also, it is critical if the physician's time is exceeded in terms of waiting. This of course is very costly and nonproductive (ie, nonvalue added).

Similar processes can be analyzed for other functions within the practice. For example, the billing process can be analyzed in such a manner, which includes consideration of the time and associated cost for charge entry, claim generation, collection process, transmission process, follow-up, mail posting, EOB posting, payment posting, and any follow-up processes, such as appeals or refunds. In the context of such an analysis, performing an appeal or refund process will at least *double* the time and associated cost of delivering the service. Thus, from a total personnel cost function, the relatively simple process of entering claims and completing the billing process is

FIGURE 3-6

Patient Encounter: Time

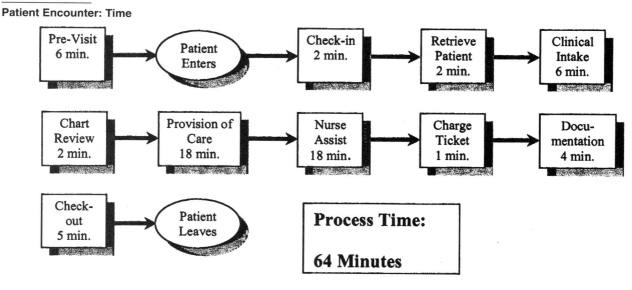

Process Time:

64 Minutes

FIGURE 3-7

Patient Encounter: Cost to Practice

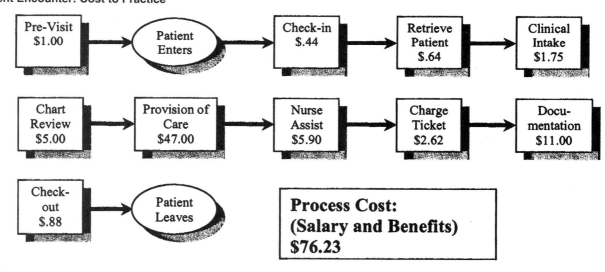

Process Cost:
(Salary and Benefits)
$76.23

increased significantly by nonvalue-added services, such as claim denial, refiling, or the processing of a refund due to an overpayment.

In this context, as we measure time, it is also a measurement of cost and, in turn, cost savings. It is important that the medical practice understand this basic concept. Every employee has a role in the continuum of services, with a cost tied to that role, both in terms of direct personnel expense and other costs, such as facilities, supplies, and so forth. Whenever the normal or targeted time required to complete a process has exceeded, the overall cost of doing business or completing that process is also significantly increased. The marginal income is reduced whenever excessive time is taken to complete the process. Thus, value-added services increase marginal income; nonvalue-added services do not.

Costs are also increased by inefficiencies. For example, if the registration or reception area is responsible for obtaining demographic information and updated insurance data, a failure to do this requires somebody else, usually at a later date, to complete this process. This additional work increases the overall cost of getting the information and results in an increase in practice expenses both in labor and in time.

SUMMARY

Expenses must be closely monitored within each medical practice. Whether expenses are isolated, based upon their direct or indirect effect, their being fixed or variable, or their difference in value due to mismanagement of time or nonvalue added services, all excessive costs result in lower margins for the practice. Maintaining a firm grasp, both directly and indirectly, on these expenses will ensure that this does not occur.

chapter 4

Assessing the Effect of Financial Performance

The key to understanding financial performance in the medical practice is to assess the effect of the operating results. Regardless of how numbers are reported (eg, on an income statement, on a balance sheet, in another form of reporting), they are meaningless in and of themselves. They must be interpreted and put into action, with changes made as a result of this review.

The backbone of the practice is its financial statement, which serves as its report card. This report card provides the answers to many questions about performance, such as:

- Who (and what) is productive
- What is the source of expenses and their relative size compared to revenue
- What is the effect of revenue, discounts, and adjustments
- Where do future opportunities lie
- What are the areas of improvement
- What is the bottom line or net income

A productivity analysis is the foundation for any evaluation process. It is also important to determine *who* is productive so appropriate action may be taken on behalf of that individual. Financial statements do not typically break down productivity by individual; however, there are many supporting reports that convey this information. Knowledge is the beginning of result. Once the sources of productivity (both high and low) are identified, they can be targeted for improvement.

The source of expenses is critically important because it must be determined if they are justifiable. (See Chapter 3 for details about the different types of expenses and how to best control them in the medical practice.) Financial interpretation of the financial statement reveals the source of these expenses. Knowing the source of expenses helps in the control of their incurrence.

The single greatest effect on financial performance in the medical practice is discounting of charges. Discounting, in some industries such as in retail, is somewhat voluntary. For example, retailers discount prices periodically to stimulate buying activity by the consumer. In health care, discounts against total standard charges are generally the result of the resolve of third-party payers to pay less for services rendered, which dramatically shapes the operating results of the medical practice or provider. When 30% to 50% of standard fees are discounted, as is typical in some markets, the profit margins drastically shrink. The financial statement exposes the significance of discounts on financial performance and their radical effect on operating performance.

A look at historical financial statements (post-period statements such as prior months, years, and so on) and consideration of the effect of these statements on overall performance reveal opportunities for future growth and expansion. For example, if a particular department demonstrates an upward trend, and the department has the capacity for additional service, these are positive indicators for the practice to consider expanding its initial investment to deliver that service. This may be an ancillary service or could be a specific procedure that is being performed by the practice. Some practices may choose to add ancillary services that complement their specialty. If the demand is there and the services are indicated for providing appropriate patient care, it may be justifiable to expand the service through promotion and increased performance of procedures. In this way, a review of financial performance, in terms of revenue and cost allocations within this service delivery (or a separate department created for this service), will unveil future opportunities.

A simple review of the financial statements promotes actions to improve operational performance. Financial statements point to areas where improvement is indicated. A financial analysis should reveal troubled departments or point to providers that are not carrying their weight. Management, at this juncture, should address the areas where improvements are needed.

Finally, the financial statements will ultimately relate to the practice's bottom line. Realizing a profit is not an unfavorable concept in the medical practice, even as part of a not-for-profit or tax-exempt entity. The practice should accumulate earnings so the business can be sustained long term. Net income or net profit, which is a worthy goal, is best illustrated on the financial statements and can be derived from individual departmental income statements, as well as the consolidated statements for the business enterprise. The financial statements are culminated in this important area of measuring their effect.

Financial statements and what they reveal enable managers and physician-owners to make immediate and future operating decisions. Over time, decisions can be made based on historical results and developing trends as indicators of the future. The following decisions can be made based on financial analysis, with obvious effects on the practice:

- Sell the practice
- Merge with another entity
- Determine the practice's fair market value
- Expand to additional locations
- Add or contract providers

Financial statements assess the future effect of the business and help formulate where that business is going. Not all historical information will dictate future decisions, though. Some will be based on other factors within the organization, including the market conditions, the physicians, their current career status, and their ability to generate revenue in a managed care environment. Nonetheless, the historical financial performance does have a major effect on these future decisions.

FIRSTHAND ANALYSIS OF THE EFFECT

The following exercise may be helpful to illustrate the need to assess the effect of the financial statements. This exercise gives several examples for conclusions from a financial statement and corresponding appropriate actions that should occur. The financial statement analysis process should involve more than simply looking at the numbers and concluding their financial effect on the bottom line. True financial statement analysis goes one step farther. It converts raw data (ie, the numbers or operating performance totals) into management decisions. Financial statements become more meaningful when they result in actions that benefit the performance of the practice.

Tables 4-1 through 4-5 illustrate the aforementioned points. The proposed actions are based on certain conclusions that might be derived from the analysis of the financial statement.

TABLE 4-1

Financial Statement Conclusion	Possible Resulting Actions
Charges growing, but not keeping pace with adjustments	■ Review payer mix
	■ Review contracts
	■ Consider alternative opportunities
	■ Adjust fee schedule
	■ Review individual provider charges
	■ Investigate procedural offering

TABLE 4-2

Financial Statement Conclusion	Possible Resulting Actions
Net collections decreasing	■ Review billing/collections process
	■ Review productivity by provider
	■ Review practice internal controls
	■ Consider prepaid (ie, capitated) payers
	■ Review facilities (eg, reduce space)
	■ Review personnel status
	■ Consider work and office hours

TABLE 4-3

Financial Statement Conclusion	Possible Resulting Actions
Office (ie, nonprovider) salaries too high and increasing	■ Consider staff realignment ■ Freeze wage increases ■ Consider incentive pay program ■ Review overtime ■ Review time off

TABLE 4-4

Financial Statement Conclusion	Possible Resulting Actions
Office supplies expense over budget and national averages	■ Review buying process ■ Review existing inventory ■ Review security of supplies

TABLE 4-5

Financial Statement Conclusion	Possible Resulting Actions
Malpractice insurance expenses in excess of budget and national averages	■ Call current carrier agent ■ Review coverages ■ Consider opening up to bid

The financial statement conclusion found in Table 4-1 is representative of many practices. The financial statement shows that, throughout a span of time, charges (ie, total gross productivity) placed on the books by the providers are increasing, yet unfortunately, adjustments (ie, contractual allowances) are climbing at a faster pace. The net charge total is actually going down or, at best, remaining stagnant. The analysis is simple and does not require an expert to draw a conclusion. What it does require, however, is a plan of action to correct the downward trend. Table 4-1 offers several obvious, yet important, alternatives for maintaining an improvement initiative.

■ **Review of payer mix.** Begin by looking at your payers as a regular initiative of the practice's management. Consider payer mix in light of developing a marketing strategy to derive a different payer mix. Marketing manifests itself in various ways for medical practices in the current payer market, including marketing that is strictly to third-party payers and, in some instances, marketing that is directly to business/industry or the patient.

■ **Contract review.** Another valid action is to review your contracts with payers. Contract renegotiation provides opportunities to increase reimbursement through improved contractual allowances.

■ **Increased innovative action.** More innovative action means that the physicians and other providers in the practice opt to perform new procedures or emphasize those that are profitable. Consider this initiative if it makes sense for your practice and specialty.

■ **Adjust the fee schedule.** Fee schedule adjustments will undoubtedly increase overall charges, yet they may also increase the overall net charge total, particularly if there are some areas where reimbursement will be accepted or certain indemnity payers will accept at or near the full fee schedule.

■ **Review individual provider charges.** Individual provider charges should be reviewed so that improvements in coding and documentation can be made.

All of these actions are based on conclusions from one financial statement review.

The remaining examples, Tables 4-2 through 4-5, further substantiate this point. These examples represent net collections, staff salaries (ie, the greatest expense), office supplies (ie, a variable expense), and malpractice insurance (ie, a major ongoing expense). Conclusions and actions are outlined briefly within each example.

The manager's responsibility is to analyze the financial statements, assess the effect of the results, and develop a plan of action for operational improvements. The action response may be formal, informal, or intuitive in accord with the manager's style and experience. Using a hands-on approach will focus the attention of the entire practice on the action plan.

OTHER INDICATORS TO WATCH

Table 4-6 encapsulates the key indicators to monitor in the medical practice. The concern in this example is organizational, yet these indicators are equally applicable for each provider or department of the practice. Most of these indicators are familiar to the seasoned practice manager. Some are more advanced and require complex record keeping, preferably from computerized output. All of these indicators are valid standards for comparing performance and useful when charted on a simple graph. The information is gathered monthly from statistics and compiled in a report. As trends develop and are charted, this report becomes a strong management tool upon which to base decisions.

MEASURES OF PRODUCTIVITY

Individual and collective provider productivity is an essential component of financial performance and has a serious effect on a medical practice. Following are some of the many ways to measure productivity:

■ Charges
  ■ Gross charges
  ■ Net charges
■ Collections

TABLE 4-6

Key Indicators to Watch

- Charge denial rate by payer and most frequent reasons
- Charges, payments, and adjustments by physician, site, and practice
- Average charge and reimbursement per patient encounter
- Number of new patients per FTE physician
- Number of capitated patients per physician
- Physician coding and medical record compliance (ie, coding trending report)
- Clinical staffing per FTE physician
- Staffing turnover rates
- Number of health professionals per FTE physician
- Number of patient encounters per allied health professional
- Billing/administrative staff per FTE physician
- Billing staff turnover ratio
- Billing staff productivity
- Average office charge entry lag
- Average inpatient charge entry lag
- Average number of missing encounter forms
- Accurate reconciliation of charge capture documents to appointment logs, hospital records, nursing home reports, and so on
- Time of service collection rate
- Collection agency collections
- Medicare waiver of compliance
- Appointment availability
- Patient wait times at time of service
- Patient cancellation rate
- Physician cancellation rate
- Number of referrals by source and/or provider

- Gross collections
- Net collections
- Visits/encounters
  - Office visits
  - Procedures
  - Consultations
  - Phone consultations
  - Hospital inpatient revenue
- Relative value units (RVUs)
  - Full RVUs
  - Work only RVUs
- Capitation
  - Covered lives
  - Available hours

There are many measurements of productivity—all valid in the medical practice, but the most practical method of measuring productivity is by outright charges generated and collected. This measure of productivity is a requirement for virtually every practice's financial performance and the analysis that results. Gross charges are defined as charges brought in before any adjustments to revenue and are not as informative as net charges or net collections (which are on a cash basis of accounting). Nonetheless, gross charges are standard and, if consistently applied across the entire practice's provider base, will lend some reliable information.

Net charges are more accurate. They reflect the number that should be collected and, therefore, reveal the true adjusted revenue figure. Collections are usually stated as a gross figure before refunds and as a net figure after refunds are issued.

Visits and patient encounters are another way to measure performance and the effect of provider productivity. Obviously, procedures performed during visits and patient encounters need to be relevant to the individual practice setting. Many practices do not perform procedures; therefore, it is not a measurement. Some practices have a variation of types of encounters, including the provision of immunizations and other ancillary procedures that would not carry the same weight or value as a regular patient encounter. All of these must be sorted and measured with their appropriate level of significance to the practice.

Relative value units are a very accurate standard with which to measure productivity performance in the practice. They are a standard, established by the government, and have been in place for many years. They are annually updated with theoretically a great deal of thought and analysis to support the values on a CPT code basis. For this reason, RVUs establish a true standard that has no relevance to actual reimbursement. This is a very accurate measure of productivity, especially in the practice with much diversity of payers from one provider to another.

RVUs are useful for comparing productivity among each provider within the medical practice. Whether they are full RVUs or work-only RVUs is irrelevant as long as they are consistently used (eg, no switching from full RVUs to work-only RVUs and vice versa during the course of the measurement periods). RVUs are often used to calculate compensation for the providers, which is a viable consideration. RVU users must make sure that certain checks and balances are in place. For example, the conversion factor (ie, the factor that converts RVUs to dollars) must be thoroughly analyzed and accurately effectuated to derive the desired compensation. Mistakes are often made in the assignment of the RVU conversion factor in a compensation plan, which will result in unfair or unbalanced compensation. Most practice management systems track RVUs and compile this data automatically, eliminating the need for the tedious manual gathering of data on an encounter-by-encounter basis per CPT-4 code by a staff member.

RVU productivity measurement also helps to assess the effect of the frequency of the procedural code. This helps providers to understand, with a well-documented patient encounter, how to properly code patient encounters. This will accumulate more RVUs (ie, presuming the encounter will be coded at a higher level of service), thus generating greater measurements of productivity.

Capitation is unique in the measurement of productivity and is often based upon a number of covered lives for the individual physician, subject to the capitated contract. These covered lives ultimately convert to a fixed dollar total, which is prepaid each month (there may also be a withhold that will be distributed later). Revenue from capitation arrangements is much easier to predict. It is, in theory, due to its nature, manageable in that there are a specific number of patients subject to this total reimbursement. Many problems result for the provider trying to manage this patient base. Historically, patients in capitation plans have had greater financial incentive to increase the number of visits, which reduces the effective productivity for each visit.

In terms of measuring productivity in a capitated plan, the practice should continue to code for services. Also, it should track services performed as if they were fee-for-service, so that productivity can be gathered based upon both charges and RVUs. Those totals can be compared to the capitated income to help assess the effect of the capitated contract. It may be that reimbursement is considerably under what it would have been in a fee-for-service environment. In this case, the true effect of discounting in this capitated contract would be dramatic. By using mechanisms such as these to measure productivity, the manager can make knowledgeable decisions about the viability of the capitated contract.

MANAGED CARE MEASURES

More restrictive forms of managed care arrangements, albeit capitated contracts, have other requirements that may or may not be directly financially related, but have significant economic effect on the practice. Such managed care measures include:

- Inpatient days
- Ancillary utilization
- Out-of-plan costs
- Protocol compliance
- Quality
- Patient satisfaction

Some of these matters are more quantitative than others. Patient satisfaction, quality, and protocol compliance may have little quantitative value, yet they are major factors of the managed care contract that must be considered by both the provider and the third-party payer.

Data that supports inpatient days, ancillary utilization, and out-of-plan costs should be regularly accumulated. This information is difficult to measure in a traditional medical practice because it is difficult to accumulate; however, most practice management software programs have tracking capabilities that can produce this data. The level of capitation in the practice should dictate the degree of emphasis to place on this information.

VARIANCE ANALYSIS

Measuring the effect of the financial performance and using a basic income statement should involve the completion of a variance analysis. A *variance analysis* is simply a proactive means to explain why certain variances have occurred between actual performance and certain comparative standards, as reported on the income statement.

The practice's income statement should have certain specific comparables (ie, standards) upon which actual performance is measured. This could be a budget or profit plan total, the prior year or even prior month total, or a certain industry benchmark. All of these could be used at different stages in the comparative analysis process. Whatever the criteria, a regular analysis should occur to explain the major differences.

A variance analysis will not consider every line item. It only considers those that significantly vary from the standard and what is significant will vary with each practice. For example, sometimes, a dollar figure of variance should be established, while at other times, the basis should be established as a percentage variance. Whatever is important and relevant to the practice should be used for the analysis.

Variance analyses are used to illustrate developing trends. Certain line items may be considered in the variance analysis where performances far exceed the plan or the prior year. These occurrences warrant an explanation. Variances are typically noted for expenses that are far above budget or for revenues that are significantly under the plan or prior year. The variances serve as red flags, signaling a need for investigation. Upon discovery, corrections can be made before it is too late in the year to have an effect.

Combined Statement of Revenue and Expenses

Excerpts from an actual variance analysis report are included and illustrated in Table 4-7, which is an example of a combined statement of revenue and expenses. This review is confined to analysis of the current month (April) for significant variance from what that month would be if trended for four months. Further review is indicated if the year-to-date total is significantly higher or lower than four times the current month.

Revenue:

- **Clinical.** The total revenue in April of $127,000 clearly exceeded those of the prior months. An analysis of this is thus appropriate. The difference may be attributable to a cash receipt matter. This is one of the fallacies of cash-based accounting.
- **Surgical.** The provision of these services was clearly down in April, totaling $100,000 less than in most months. This should be researched.
- **Pathology lab.** In April, lab work increased, which does not necessarily flow with the fact that surgical work was down.

TABLE   4-7

Combined Statement of Revenue and Expenses

Revenues	Current Month (April)	%	Year to Date	%
Clinical	127,484.67	46.04	550,100.53	43.87
Unposted Credits	−3,587.41	−1.30	11,517.59	0.92
Surgical	82,869.65	29.93	445,043.35	35.49
Pathology Lab	48,170.93	17.40	176,482.09	14.08
Aesthetics	18,734.69	6.77	58,158.67	4.64
Skin Care Products	3,822.89	1.38	14,599.46	1.16
Phototherapy	3,898.60	1.41	19,125.21	1.53
Refunds	−4,471.70	−1.61	−21,204.41	−1.69
Total Revenue	**276,922.32**	**100.00**	**1,253,822.49**	**100.00**
Physician Expenses				
Salary	65,179.00	23.54	227,901.78	18.18
Bonus	142,375.00	51.41	142,375.00	11.36
Payroll Taxes	8,739.09	3.16	21,487.77	1.71
Retirement	0.00	0.00	9,843.81	0.79
401K (company match)	0.00	0.00	6,724.26	0.54
Salary (PA)	5,138.46	1.86	19,630.79	1.57
Payroll Taxes (PA)	393.09	0.14	1,554.22	0.12
Auto Expense	1,554.66	0.56	3,471.82	0.28
Auto Lease	764.97	0.28	3,059.88	0.24
Cell Phone	286.40	0.10	1,191.10	0.09
Cont Ed and Seminars	0.00	0.00	50.00	0.00
Dues and Subscriptions	331.18	0.12	5,984.58	0.48
Fees and License	0.00	0.00	1,500.00	0.12
Insurance (health)	317.83	0.11	1,271.32	0.10
Insurance (life)	1,442.24	0.52	6,059.78	0.48
Insurance (prof liability)	−274.00	−0.10	3,916.00	0.31
Meals	47.50	0.02	343.90	0.03
Misc Expense	1,605.00	0.58	1,880.12	0.15
Travel	0.00	0.00	4,088.42	0.33
Uniforms	22.73	0.01	73.69	0.01
Total Physician Expenses	**227,923.15**	**82.31**	**462,408.24**	**36.88**
Operating Expenses				
Salary	40,415.35	14.59	159,404.56	12.71
Payroll Taxes	3,954.28	1.43	12,194.45	0.97
Retirement	0.00	0.00	4,117.81	0.33
401K (company match)	0.00	0.00	2,160.61	0.17
Film and Developing	41.48	0.01	127.81	0.01
Insurance (health)	2,381.99	0.86	9,609.21	0.77
Medical Supplies	14,646.96	5.29	63,160.95	5.04
Professional Services	21.25	0.01	366.25	0.03
Merchandise	3,952.65	1.43	5,646.19	0.45
Merchandise Discarded	0.00	0.00	281.50	0.02
Repairs and Maintenance	109.00	0.04	734.95	0.06
Total Operating Expenses	**65,522.96**	**23.66**	**257,804.29**	**20.56**

Revenues	Current Month (April)	%	Year to Date	%
Administrative Expenses				
Accounting	0.00	0.00	6,050.00	0.48
Advertising	712.55	0.26	4,048.65	0.32
Auto Lease (company car)	428.04	0.15	428.04	0.03
Auto Expense	0.00	0.00	116.96	0.01
Bank Charges	250.14	0.09	562.44	0.04
Credit Card Fees	493.24	0.18	2,423.35	0.19
Charitable Contributions	975.00	0.35	4,800.00	0.38
Dues and Subscriptions	402.94	0.15	5,080.73	0.41
Consulting	4,512.00	1.63	4,685.20	0.37
Cont Ed and Seminars	2,721.00	0.98	2,896.00	0.23
Computer Support and Maintenance	1,067.80	0.39	1,067.80	0.09
Employee Relations	547.81	0.20	2,016.55	0.16
Entertainment	61.79	0.02	5,459.84	0.44
Equipment Lease	8,087.09	2.92	41,116.64	3.28
Equipment Services Contract	0.00	0.00	4,108.36	0.33
Insurance (general)	195.00	0.07	344.00	0.03
Insurance (health)	535.86	0.19	1,566.98	0.12
Insurance (prof liability)	132.00	0.05	179.00	0.01
Insurance (workers comp)	0.00	0.00	1,401.00	0.11
Interest Expense	4,917.60	1.78	20,877.71	1.67
Lawn Maintenance	469.81	0.17	469.81	0.04
Legal Fees	0.00	0.00	1,589.98	0.13
License and Fees	0.00	0.00	1,185.00	0.09
Marketing	1,229.20	0.44	3,534.38	0.28
Misc Expense	1,786.77	0.65	4,022.38	0.32
Office Supplies	3,311.26	1.20	9,779.64	0.78
Outside Service	5,915.90	2.14	14,744.77	1.18
Patient Education	0.00	0.00	533.40	0.04
Postage	262.90	0.09	3,314.18	0.26
Printing	3,036.42	1.10	7,786.44	0.62
Recruiting	233.75	0.08	233.75	0.02
Reference Materials	−54.06	−0.02	842.00	0.07
Rent	21,913.33	7.91	87,653.32	6.99
Repairs and Maintenance	414.86	0.15	2,822.04	0.23
Returned Checks	175.60	0.06	186.05	0.01
Salary	12,800.51	4.62	47,860.67	3.82
Payroll Taxes	1,392.78	0.50	5,924.77	0.47
Retirement	0.00	0.00	-4,024.07	-0.32
401K (company match)	0.00	0.00	616.60	0.05
Sales Tax	887.70	0.32	1,670.49	0.13
Taxes (other)	0.00	0.00	10,987.56	0.88
Telephone	1,580.48	0.57	6,473.94	0.52
Travel	3,391.69	1.22	4,528.69	0.36
Uniforms	260.14	0.09	420.52	0.03
Utilities	3,840.04	1.39	8,108.05	0.65
Total Administrative Expense	**88,888.94**	**32.10**	**330,493.61**	**26.36**

continued

TABLE 4-7 *continued*

Combined Statement of Revenue and Expenses

Revenues	Current Month (April)	%	Year to Date	%
Other Income and Expenses				
Other Income	50.00	0.02	425.00	0.03
Amort Exp (startup)	−83.33	−0.03	−333.32	−0.03
Amort Exp (software)	−3,754.17	−1.36	−15,016.68	−1.20
Amort Exp (organization costs)	−52.67	−0.02	−210.68	−0.02
Amort Exp (goodwill)	−133.33	−0.05	−533.32	−0.04
Deprec Exp (computer)	−5,146.75	−1.86	−20,587.00	−1.64
Deprec Exp (equipment)	−11,200.58	−4.04	−44,802.32	−3.57
Deprec Exp (furniture and fixtures)	−1,366.83	−0.49	−5,467.32	−0.44
Total Other Income/Exp	**−21,687.66**	**−7.83**	**−86,525.64**	**−6.90**
Excess (Deficit)	**−127,100.39**	**−45.90%**	**116,590.71**	**9.30%**
Revenue Over Expenses				

- **Aesthetics.** This service was also up in April. Research of this is needed.
- **Total revenue.** The overall trend of total revenue was down in April. For the first three months of the year, revenue averaged more than $325,000. In April, it was approximately $277,000. As noted above, this could be attributable to something as simple as the performance of collections. It could also be due to the fact that, in some practices, collections are deferred until the new year to lessen the amount of income taxes to be paid in the prior year. Nonetheless, research to provide answers to these variances should take place.

Physician expenses:

- **Salary.** As a percent of revenue, this was much higher for April (ie, 5% greater than year to date, for a total of 18%). This is due to lower revenue and illustrates the problems caused by decreased revenue.
- **Bonus.** This apparently is the quarterly bonus month. The bonus is paid each April, July, October, and January. However, given that the current month's amount is the same as the year-to-date, it can be determined that the January bonus was not paid. Explanation of this should be pursued. Aside from this, we recommend a different presentation for the bonuses. This should follow the bottom line on the financial statement. We have recommended that physician expenses be the last section of the income statement. Even below this, however, would appear physician bonuses so that a net bottom line would be illustrated. Prior to that, a net bottom line would also be illustrated before physician bonuses. This would have greater integrity in relation to the percentages as they are listed on the income statement. We recommend this be applied for each of the statements.

- **Retirement and 401(k) company match.** No entries were made in April; however, there are year-to-date balances.
- **Miscellaneous expense.** Miscellaneous expense is always a catch-all, but needs to be explained as to its content. For example, in April it was more than $1,600; that is greater than one-half of 1%.

Operating expenses:

- **Insurance.** Insurance premiums were down slightly in April compared to prior months.
- **Medical supplies.** Compared to prior months, medical supply costs were down slightly.
- **Merchandise.** In April, the merchandise expense was up, comprising $4,000 of the $5,600 year-to-date. Obviously, a purchase of merchandise was made, which further skews the financial statement.

Administrative expenses:

- **Advertising.** This expense was considerably down in April.
- **Auto lease, company car.** There was only one entry result for the auto lease, and that was in April.
- **Dues and subscriptions.** The expense for dues and subscriptions was considerably down in April.
- **Consulting.** Virtually all consulting was realized in April. Is this valid?
- **Continuing education and seminars.** Virtually all of this expense was also incurred in April. Is this accurate?
- **Computer support and maintenance.** All of this expense was incurred in April. Again, is this reasonable?
- **Equipment lease.** This expense was considerably down in April. What occurred to cause this to be at least $5,000 to $8,000 less? It appears that one extra month's payment was possibly made for this lease this year.
- **Equipment service contract.** No charge occurred on the equipment service contract in April. Is this because it was not paid?
- **Miscellaneous expenses, office supplies, and outside services.** Each of these expenses was considerably up in April. An explanation of these charges should be pursued.
- **Printing.** Printing in April comprises almost half of the year-to-date total. This should be explained.
- **Repairs and maintenance.** Presumably because no repair or maintenance occurred, this expense was down in April.
- **Retirement.** While there is no entry for April, the current year-to-date shows a $4,000 credit balance. What is the explanation for this?
- **Travel.** Travel expenses were up considerably in April. We presume it ties to the continuing education increase. Nonetheless, explanations of this should be completed.

This analysis illustrates how key items should be considered and what their potential effect is on the operating performance of the practice. A significant function of financial management is to target these items for explanation from the financial statement analysis and to document them in the variance report. A true variance analysis would be based upon comparatives against prior years' income statements and/or budget for both the current month and the year to date.

THE EFFECT OF FINANCIAL STATEMENTS ON LONG-TERM FINANCIAL MANAGEMENT ISSUES

As the practice develops its strategies for the future, the ramifications of the decisions made on long-term financial management issues become an important factor. Measuring the effect of current financial performance on decisions for the future is an exercise that must be regularly completed. Certain strategies or actions that have a long-term financial effect on the practice should also be considered in this process. Examples of long-term strategies include adding a new provider (or mid-level provider), adding new equipment (ie, computer systems), buying supplies, and selecting vendors. Other aspects to consider are making improvements to coding procedures and adding or contracting locations, facilities, and so forth. In measuring the effect of the financial performance on such actions, it is important to remember that in some instances the return on investment may be over a longer period of time and may not even be realized until the first year after the investment has been made. For example, whenever an existing practice decides to add another physician, it is highly likely that the operating results will suffer during that individual's first year. The existing physicians may experience a decrease in compensation and will have lower operating margins. The time that it takes to bring the new physician up to a sufficient level of productivity normally extends over a significant period, often more than one year. Practice decisions, such as bringing on a new associate, must be made with the knowledge that it will take time to justify the decision from a fiscal standpoint, due to front-end reductions in operating margins and income. Initially, adding a new associate would not appear to have been a wise decision unless it is regarded as an investment made over time that will be justified once the new physician reaches capacity. The investment in an additional physician will strengthen the practice in its fiscal viability in the long-term.

The same situation often takes place in a cost-benefit analysis when purchasing equipment, expanding facilities, or in other areas where major strategic decisions are contemplated. The financial analysis should depict the effect of this decision over an extended period of time. Ultimately, it should show a justifiable return on investment; otherwise, the decision would be inappropriate.

The best way to analyze expenses is to define the additional costs for completing the investment. For example, the costs for adding a new provider are fairly predictable, with the greatest expense being salary and benefits. Likewise, supporting the new physician will generate additional costs for support staff and other assets, such as computers and other administrative costs. Space needs may or may not be a consideration, depending upon whether the new physician can use existing space in the facility. These are a combination of both fixed (or semi-fixed comprising the majority of the total) and some variable expenses that will only be incurred as the additional revenue is produced. Those will then be compared to the projections of revenue that the new individual would be expected to complete.

Chapter 7 explores the entire process of evaluating the effect of major decisions on financial operations. For this chapter, however, Table 4-8 illustrates the various ways to quantify the analysis of the practice's decision—in this example, the addition of a new mid-level provider (MLP). The analysis is basically set up in three columns: (1) before adding the MLP, (2) the effect of adding the MLP, and (3) after the MLP addition combined with other practice operations. The example illustrates all the components of this relationship, both variable and fixed. The final analysis, an expected margin, is calculated. This, in effect, is the long-term return on investment that is anticipated from this venture. It is a combination of fixed and variable expenses as well as the additional effect on revenues that will be considered in comparison to those additional costs.

CAPITAL ACQUISITION AND INVESTMENT SCENARIOS

There are different alternatives for capital acquisition, usually attained through debt financing or equity partnering. Each has its advantages and disadvantages. Debt financing may be sourced through commercial banks, finance companies, insurance companies, leasing entities, and health care specialty lenders. Equity capital is derived from venture capitalists, physician groups, hospitals, and other related health care entities.

The decision to raise capital through debt versus equity poses an age-old dilemma for the borrower. From the debt-financing standpoint, the *partner* is the lender and is satisfied with the

T A B L E   4-8

Effect Analysis

	Before MLP	Net Financial Effect of MLP	After MLP
1. Projected visits	5,500	3,500	9,000
2. Collections	$300,000	$200,000	$500,000
3. Total fixed costs (cash)	$110,000	$70,000	$180,000
4. Total fixed costs (noncash)	$5,000	$2,000	$7,000
5. Total variable costs	$30,000	$15,000	$45,000
6. Physician compensation (total)	$140,000	$0	$140,000
7. Total expenses (add lines 3 through 6)	$285,000	$87,000	$372,000
8. Net income (line 2 minus line 7)	$15,000	$113,000	$128,000
Additional noncash expenses	$5,000	$2,000	$7,000
Cash available	$20,000	$115,000	$135,000

investment as long as the debt is repaid and the requirements of the loan are met. The lender's return on investment is limited to the interest that the debt will yield, with no further expectations.

In comparison, equity partnering to raise capital introduces potential problems arising from expectations for prospective performance. Although the partner is not guaranteed a return on investment, the risk is in the investor's expectations to exceed what interest would yield. The original partner does not consider the equity partner's involvement a requirement to perform at a specific level, while the new partner expects a yield that exceeds a return from interest. The disparity in expectations can often be problematic.

Furthermore, the equity partner's stake in the ownership of the business allows for some say-so in its management, operations, and organization. With sufficient equity, the new partner could effect changes in the oversight of the practice. This is a factor that must not be overlooked when considering fundraising options. The equity partner expects, although is not guaranteed, a return on investment and a right to be heard in management, even when holding a minority interest. In most cases, the lender's expectations will not require a voice in management issues, but will require assurance that the borrower will repay the debt and service the interest on an ongoing basis. In most cases, the equity partner will want a larger return through a sale or merger, which will require the other owners to be willing to sell the business or to engage in a new ownership arrangement.

Typically, health care practices use both equity and debt to raise capital, depending on the nature of the business and the preferences of the equity partners. In a practice start-up, the partner will almost always have to be another physician. The question is whether the physician will be able to bring capital to the practice or just function as a potential owner, producing revenue as opposed to contributing funds. With other ventures, such as an ambulatory surgery centers, using outside venture capital may make the most sense. The trade-off is in division of interests in profit sharing and decision-making responsibilities.

An outright practice acquisition will probably require a combination of debt and equity in the business, depending upon the practice makeup, after the acquisition occurs. If one physician acquires the practice from another, it is likely that the acquiring physician will either borrow the money or invest his or her own funds from savings and other sources. Options for financing this transaction include allowing the selling physician to finance the purchase by accepting payment on account over a period of time.

Equipment purchases are financed through debt, whether it be by short-, long-, or intermediate-term financing, depending upon the price of the equipment. Most equipment will require short- or intermediate-term financing, normally five years or less. Long-term debt is used to purchase major equipment or real estate. Capital for major ventures, such as surgery centers, diagnostic centers, infusion centers, walk-in clinics, and so on, is raised through a combination of means, including both debt and equity.

Depending upon the nature of the investment, different scenarios require individual evaluation and understanding to come up with longer-term capital financing. All facets of equity arrangements, such as giving up ownership and sharing potential earnings, should be considered in light of their effect on the practice and will have a lot to do with the outcome of the investment.

Generally, debt financing is categorized based on the terms of the loan, as follows:

- Short-term loans are for working capital needs
- Intermediate-term loans are usually for non-major equipment
- Long-term loans are typically for buildings, property, and large multi-thousand dollar equipment
- Equity sharing or true partnerships occurs when there is a desire to spread the risk, the ability to borrow is perhaps less than favorable, and the need for assistance in management, organization, building, and maintenance is greater (ie, the need for a true operating partner is greater than the actual need for source of funds)

Leasing agreements, another alternative to financing, are one of two types of arrangements: (1) operating lease or (2) capital lease. The *operating lease* provides no opportunity for ownership, either at the beginning or during the term of the lease. It essentially says that payments are due as leases are due, on a regular basis with no residual value going to the lessee in the leased property asset. A *capital lease,* conversely, conveys the ability for the lessee to realize ownership. Various capital leases call for different ownership, depending upon the terms of the lease. Some capital leases will call for conversion of ownership at the beginning of the lease, which is similar to an actual loan. Other capital leases will call for a fair market value buyout, depending upon the asset's full value at the end of the lease. Still others will require a nominal buyout at the end of the lease, which essentially says that this type of lease has been a capital financing vehicle all along.

The following are the advantages and disadvantages to leasing arrangements.

Advantages to leasing:

- Capital leases are 100% tax deductible and offer the option of 100% financing. Capital leases require little, if any, money down on the financing of the equipment in comparison with a loan that normally requires a down payment toward the asset being acquired.
- Operating leases will limit the risk of obsolescence. Once the lease expires, the asset may be replaced with a new piece of equipment through a new lease.
- Leases do not necessarily get to the balance sheet and will help with certain existing ratios or credit indicators.

Disadvantages to leasing:

- The cost of leasing generally will exceed traditional financing. At higher effective interest rates, leasing may not be justifiable.

- A straight operating lease allows the lessee no benefit of ownership. Capital leases provide the opportunity for ownership, but perhaps at a higher interest rate than a traditional loan.

SUMMARY

In analyzing the effect of financial statements on the medical practice and other health care entities, it is important to stay focused on the overall financial results of the practice's business operations. Simply reviewing financial statements for the sake of reviewing them and summarizing operating results has little if any benefit to the manager until it is translated into credible information and transferred to viable decisions for the business and its future. Making appropriate decisions is a key part of managing and owning a health care entity. The success of a medical practice, a surgery center, or some other enterprise largely depends upon the owner's ability to detect trends as they occur and to assess the overall effect on future financial performance.

Ratios and Benchmarking

This chapter presents two important components of successful financial analysis and management within the medical practice: ratios and benchmarks. Ratios and benchmarks can be used as quick and concise methods for determining performance. They do not require extensive and detailed analysis of a financial statement, which is more intricate. Moreover, they provide quick determinants of performance that allow the manager, as well as the physician-owner, to take quick action.

RATIOS

Simply stated, *ratios* are methods of testing relationships with each other (ie, the comparisons of one number to another). In a financial arena, ratios typically are comparisons of performance measurements within the two major financial statements—the income statement and the balance sheet. Certain ratios are comparisons of two income statement items, while others compare an income statement item versus the balance sheet, and still others compare to balance sheet items.

Ratios are used to evaluate the performance of a medical practice. They are a key to financial analysis. There are several different types of ratios that can be considered as important measurement tools when determining the outcomes and ongoing performance of various components of the practice. For example, ratios that are related to the performance of accounts receivable correspond to the activities and general productivity of the billing department. Ratios that relate to overhead correspond to administration and operations and the proficiency of this area of the practice's management. Ratios pertaining to revenue respond to the performance of the providers and are relative to their individual practices.

Key Revenue and Expense Ratios

The practice should consider researching and reviewing the key ratios that are listed below; however, bear in mind, the following list is not complete, there are many other ratios that could be evaluated. Likewise, some of the following ratios should be evaluated in greater detail or separated on a departmental basis (ie, the same ratio that is reviewed for the whole practice may be used for determining performance within an individual department or division within the practice). Important key ratios include:

- Collection ratio
- Days of revenue and accounts receivable
- Visits per provider per day
- Collections per provider
- Nonmedical staff members per provider
- Total staffing per provider
- Practice overhead percentage
- Occupancy expenses per provider
- Average revenue per patient
- Average cost per patient
- No-shows versus scheduled appointments
- Physician cancellation rate
- Collection agency and rate of charges
- Payer mix ratios
- Marketing costs per new patient
- Departmental expense ratios

Methods of calculating these ratios are fairly obvious. The following are a few examples of how to go about the calculating process for various key ratios.

Collection Ratio

The collection ratio simply determines how much, in the way of charges, has been collected in the practice's bank account. The collection ratio can be calculated using both total (or gross) charges, as well as net (or adjusted) charges. Then the ratio can be shown under this to indicate gross (or unadjusted) collections ratio equals total collections divided by total gross charges. The net (or adjusted) collection ratio equals total collections divided by total net charges. One of the advantages of using ratios is to quickly determine performance. The process of ratio analysis requires going beyond the sheer mathematics to discern what is actually occurring. The objective of the review is to discover opportunities for improvement within the practice's performance. The goal, in the context of the collection ratios, is to derive a standard by looking at the total dollars that are collected versus gross charges. Because it is highly unlikely that a practice collects its gross charges, an analysis of gross charges does not reflect an exact representation of performance. The analysis will show that, assuming the standard fee schedule is used month-to-month, a constant collection ratio indicates a measure of consistency and overall performance from one month to another. However, the adjusted collection ratio is very informative about how well the practice is performing. The adjusted collection ratio says that the practice has collected a certain amount relative to what should have been collected (ie, net charges). Although there is a difference in timing of the charges being collected today versus those placed on the books at a later date, a collection ratio clearly relates a percentage of such performance relative to adjusted charges.

From an interpretive standpoint, a net collection ratio of 90% is not the optimum. This is saying that out of every dime that should have been collected, nine cents is being collected. From a management viewpoint, the accounts receivable is increasing. When this happens, working capital is decreasing and the practice is borrowing money or will not be able to pay its own physicians the anticipated compensation.

A brief monthly ratio report is a source of information for the physicians and administrators to use as a tool for making decisions for operational improvement. For example, a consistent net or adjusted collection ratio of less than 100% from month to month indicates that the receivables balance is increasing and working capital or cash flow is not as good as it should have been. This ratio may be acceptable for a practice that is growing, but it is not acceptable for one that is fairly stable and predictable. The attractiveness of using a ratio is its quick and concise determination of performance, which can result in a swift management decision on what needs to be done to improve the billing and collections process.

Days Outstanding in Accounts Receivable Ratio

Other accounts receivable ratios are available and important for interpretive use, such as analyzing the days outstanding in accounts receivable. An analysis of days outstanding in accounts receivable is a determination of the average amount of discounted charges billed over a defined period, perhaps three months. The average accounts receivable should be no more than a certain amount that encompasses these average monthly discounted charges. The following formula or ratio is used to determine if there is outstanding revenue in accounts receivable:

Adjusted charges for the last three months ÷
Total number of days for the same period =
Average adjusted revenue per day

Outstanding adjusted accounts receivable ÷
Average adjusted revenue per day =
Days in accounts receivable

When the calculation is completed, the end result is the number of days in accounts receivable. For example, if the average adjusted charges for the last three months were $270,000 and the total outstanding balance was $300,000, the calculation would be as follows:

$270,000 ÷ 90 days = $3,000 average adjusted revenue

$300,000 ÷ $3,000 = 100 days in A/R

As another example of what can be realized from a simple ratio calculation, the interpretive phase of this says that 100 days in accounts receivable as of today means it would take 100 days to collect this balance. This means that more than three months or 100 days of working capital is required to maintain this practice's cash flow needs. This, of course, is an excessive period and will put greater than normal fiscal stress on the practice.

The days outstanding in accounts receivable may be considered based upon either gross or net charges and receivable balance. It is easier to use a gross charge title because most accounts receivable balances in the medical practice are stated at gross (ie, the accounts receivable is adjusted at the time payment is received). This is acceptable as long as the understanding is that the number of days outstanding represents the gross total and thus, at any given time, accounts receivable is overstated, including the balance represented in the number of days. Preferably (and therefore recommended), this ratio will be used to derive an adjusted charge total. It is easy to derive adjusted charges for the amount or period being measured, but it may be more difficult to adjust accounts receivable in the numerator of the above fraction. However, with history on the side of most practices, it will be relatively easy to take the outstanding accounts receivable and apply a percentage adjustment that is comparable to the contractual allowance and bad debt rate for that practice, thus deriving an adjusted outstanding accounts receivable balance. If used, then the number of days outstanding in accounts receivable would reflect the adjusted ratio, which would also provide better information under the circumstances.

It is essential to have the capability to quickly determine performance. Most physicians do not want to have to comb through extensive information and data in order to make decisions, nor do busy administrators. Yet, paperwork must be reviewed due to the critical nature of the accounts receivable/billing and collection process for the successful management of the practice. Ratios that are accurately and consistently calculated and supplied to administration and the owners of the practice on a regular basis will enable decision-makers to quickly discern performance.

Ratios provide an opportunity for beneficial management decisions. Why do the accounts receivable get so old before anything is addressed or changed in the practice? Often, the answer is because ratios, where trends can be tracked, are not used.

For example, take the previous ratio of days in accounts receivable formula. Review that ratio on a monthly basis, graphed in such a way that illustrates the total number of days outstanding over the past six months. This graph could allow a quick yet decisive conclusion that accounts receivable was consistently at a higher than acceptable level. Even worse, it might indicate that they are increasing at an unacceptable level. This would immediately trigger actions for improvement.

Expense-to-Earnings Ratio

Another viable ratio in the medical practice is that of overhead relative to revenue, which can take various forms depending upon how revenue is to be calculated and defined. One example would be simply the practice overhead percentage, also known as the expense to earnings ratio. This is a simple formula, as follows:

Total operating expenses (less provider salaries and benefits) ÷ Total revenue = Practice overhead to revenue

In the numerator of this ratio, total operating expenses are generally all those expenses consisting of overhead, except for the physicians' and other providers' salaries and benefits. The best method for presenting financial statements is reviewed and illustrated in Chapter 1. In this regard, it separates revenue less expenses prior to any physician compensation to derive a gross operating margin before considering any provider compensation, benefits, and other perks. Thus, this is the numerator of this ratio. The denominator is total revenue. Again, revenue can be defined in different ways. On a cash basis of accounting, revenue is probably most relevant for the use of this ratio for total collections. For other practices, revenue may be net charges or even gross charges. The recommended is net charges because gross charges are most often not reflective of real-world happenings within the practice.

Other expense-to-revenue ratios also exist. Usually, these are simply components of the overhead, broken down into their individual department or account summary. For example, the following ratio would apply if considering total personnel overhead to revenue:

Total personnel expense ÷ Total revenue = Personnel expense to revenue

This gives total personnel expense to total revenue and, once again, is a quick determinant of practice performance.

In considering benchmarking later in this chapter, this personnel expense to total revenue will become even more relevant as most of these ratios are used to compare to standards within the industry. Thus, a personnel ratio within the practice of 25% is generally within benchmark standards and an acceptable level for most practices. Keep in mind that personnel expense, by definition, includes more than salaries (eg, salaries, benefits, and other perquisites, such as retirement plans). When this ratio is analyzed from month to month, it indicates trends that are potentially relevant to determining when expenses are acceptable and when they are not.

Staffing Ratio

Other determinates of the performance of a practice may not even involve actual dollars. For example, the staffing ratio is as follows:

Total number of FTEs ÷ Total number of providers = Staffing ratio

Generally, staffing ratios regarding full-time equivalent (FTE) employees consider both employees on staff and the actual providers, which would include mid-level providers (MLP) also. (Providers are defined as those that are generating professional fees of some proportion.) Some practices will dilute the status of nonphysician providers, thus reducing their FTE weight, because there is lower expectations for productivity for nonphysician providers than for physicians. This ratio, nevertheless, provides a definitive depiction of the practice's operations as they relate to staff and providers. Later in this chapter when looking at benchmarks, it will become apparent that this ratio is a major benchmarking comparison by-product.

A ratio of 3.0 FTE staff employees to each provider simply indicates that there are three employees for every provider (ie, physician or nonphysician provider). This helps to relate to the practice's operations and also to determine the actual dollars that are expended versus the number of employees in the practice.

Visit/Encounter Ratios

Other ratios tell how performance has occurred relative to number of visits or patient encounters. For example, average revenue per patient formula is simply as follows:

$$Total\ monthly\ revenue \div Total\ patient\ visits =$$
$$Average\ revenue\ per\ patient$$

This ratio can be broken down by provider, department, or any way the practice deems appropriate. The definition of the numerator (ie, monthly revenue) will also vary (eg, gross charges, net charges, even actual collections).

In addition, costs can be measured on a per patient basis, as the following examples point out:

$$Expenses\ per\ month\ (excluding\ physician\ salaries\ and\ benefits) \div$$
$$Total\ patient\ visits$$

and

$$Expenses\ per\ month\ (including\ physician\ salaries) \div$$
$$Total\ patient\ visits$$

This ratio provides an early warning signal to the analyzer of the performance of the practice, as an indicator of the costs on a per patient basis, both before and after consideration of provider salaries and benefits. If expenses per visit are too high and are consistently increasing, the margins will continue to decrease.

RVU Ratios

Another way of defining revenue could be in the form of relative value units (RVUs). Thus, average RVUs per patient could be another ratio to use with the aforementioned formula, but changed to accommodate a numerator for RVUs. For example:

$$Total\ patient\ encounters \div Total\ RVUs =$$
$$Average\ RVUs\ per\ patient\ encounter$$

Or by procedure:

Total RVUs for procedures ÷ Total number of procedures =
Average RVUs per procedure

Unit or Departmental Ratios

Costs can also be broken down on a unit or departmental basis. For example, if a laboratory exists within a practice, the following ratio could result:

Total expenses for lab ÷ Total charges for all CPT codes related to lab test
= Lab expenses to lab revenue

This ratio tells the reader the contribution of the laboratory versus its expenses.

Payer Mix Ratio

Payer mix is another important ratio to consider in the medical practice. A typical payer mix ratio would be based upon net charges for a payer, divided by total net charges for the practice. Thus, if Medicare comprises $50,000 of a $100,000 total net charge, the Medicare payer mix is 50%.

Payer mix can also be stated in the form of a ratio relative to encounters. Thus, in the same example, if the practice had 1,000 visits in the period and 400 of them were Medicare, the Medicare ratio based upon number of patients would be 40% Medicare.

In summary, ratios are critical to the successful management of the medical practice. They are quick and to the point, but what they reveal is very insightful. The practice administrator should use ratios regularly (ie, at least monthly, if not more often) and submit them to the physician-owners for decisive information. Ratios should be based on unvarying criteria and consistently applied so that they maintain credibility. For example, do not use a collection ratio based upon gross charges in one month and then upon net charges in the next—the two are inconsistent.

Table 5-1 summarizes the key financial analysis ratios that should be considered within the medical practice. Examples are also included for ease of understanding. A practice should develop and submit a flash report of key ratios as a part of the management reporting process each month. This succinct report of ratios (likely just one or two pages) will be very revealing, and over time, with regular use, likely will be one of the most important components of the financial analysis process.

Key Credit Ratios

The previous ratios are important to the financial analysis of the medical practice, yet other ratios—especially those related to credit indicators and credit worthiness of the medical practice—should also be considered on an overall basis within the practice. Physicians are often stymied by their ability to borrow capital without

TABLE 5-1

Key Financial Analysis Ratios

Collection Ratio

$$\frac{\text{Total collections}}{\text{Total gross charges}} = \text{gross (unadjusted) collection ratio}$$

$$\frac{\$90,000}{\$150,000} = 60\%$$

$$\frac{\text{Total collections}}{\text{Total net charges}} = \text{Net (adjusted) collection ratio}$$

$$\frac{\$90,000}{\$100,000} = 90\%$$

Days in Accounts Receivable

$$\frac{\text{Adjusted charges for the last three (3) months}}{\text{Total number of days (for same period)}} = \text{Average adjusted revenue per day}$$

$$\frac{\$270,000}{90 \text{ days}} = \$3,000 \text{ average adjusted revenue per day}$$

$$\frac{\text{Outstanding net accounts receivable*}}{\text{Average adjusted revenue per day}} = \text{Days in accounts receivable}$$

$$\frac{\$300,000}{\$3,000} = 100 \text{ days in accounts receivable}$$

*Apply a typical adjustment percentage to outstanding accounts receivable to derive net accounts receivable.

Practice Overhead Percentage (aka, Expense to Earnings Ratio)

$$\frac{\text{Total Operating Expenses (less physician salaries and benefits)}}{\text{Total collections}} = \text{Practice Overhead Percentage}$$

$$\frac{\$60,000}{\$90,000} = 66.7\%$$

Expense as a Percentage of Collections

$$\frac{\text{Total personnel expense}}{\text{Total collections}} = \text{Personnel expense ratio}$$

$$\frac{\$20,000}{\$90,000} = 22.2\%$$

Staffing Ratio

$$\frac{\text{Total number of FTE employees}}{\text{Total number of FTE providers}} = \text{Staffing ratio}$$

$$\frac{10 \text{ FTE employees}}{3 \text{ FTE providers}} = 22.2\%$$

Average Revenue Per Patient

$$\frac{\text{Total monthly collections}}{\text{Total patient visits}} = \text{Average revenue per patient}$$

$$\frac{\$90,000}{90} = \$100$$

Average Cost Per Patient (Two Methods)

$$\frac{\text{Expenses per month (excluding physician salaries and benefits)}}{\text{Total patient visits}} =$$

$$\text{Average cost per patient}$$

$$\frac{\$50,000}{900} = \$55.56$$

$$\frac{\text{Expenses per month (including physician salaries and benefits)}}{\text{Total patient visits}} =$$

$$\text{Average cost per patient}$$

$$\frac{\$100,000}{900} = \$111.11$$

Departmental Expense Ratios

$$\frac{\text{Total expenses for laboratory for period}}{\text{Total net charges for all CPT codes related to laboratory tests}} =$$

$$\text{Laboratory departmental expense ratio}$$

$$\frac{\$15,000}{\$25,000} = 60\%$$

Payer Mix Ratios

$$\frac{\text{Each payer's net charges*}}{\text{Total net charges*}} = \text{Payer mix ratio}$$

$$\frac{\$20,000}{\$100,000} = 20\%$$

*Could also be completed on a "gross" basis, assuming the same fee schedule is applied or utilized for all payers.

providing their own personal guarantee. Competent managers should help physicians realize that certain key credit indicators should be present in order to be able to borrow; for instance, this could include the practice's capability to retain earnings and not distribute all earnings to its owners. Initially, not distributing all profits to the owners may appear to have a negative tax implication, yet this is not necessarily so. For example, via a pass-through of net income scenario (ie, subject to a Sub-S corporation, limited liability company, or partnership), a practice can retain earnings by simply distributing enough monies for the owners to pay their individual income taxes at their respective rates, usually 40% or less.

In considering key credit indicator ratios, the net income of the business and/or retained earnings has significant effect on the credit worthiness of the practice and the physician-owners' subsequent ability to borrow money as opposed to providing their personal guarantees. Table 5-2 highlights key credit indicators and target requirements that creditors examine.

The key credit indicators of the above ratios consider debt, equity, and liquidity. The first ratio, debt service coverage, simply indicates an amount of income (ie, after physician compensation but before noncash and non-operating items, such as depreciation and debt service) in comparison to the principal and interest payments on the loan. The prospective lender would like to have at least one-and-one-half times the principal and interest payments in bottom line net income, which is another reason why many medical practices are starting to retain some of their earnings and not distribute all of the profits to the owners. A history of continual retained income in the practice provides assurance to lenders that the practice maintains sufficient funds to cover principal and interest payments.

The next ratio, debt to capitalization, is all debt divided by debt plus equity. This is a strong basis for the argument of retaining earnings in the business (although the amount does not have to be significant). The targeted ratio is 75% or less, as indicated in Table 5-2. Therefore, the debt should not be more than 75% of the total debt plus equity.

Return on equity is quite simple to understand. It is the net income divided by the equity at both the beginning and end of the year divided by two. This allows a lender to realize a comfort level based upon ongoing profitability. Thus, in order to meet the first three key credit indicators, a medical practice would have to maintain some level of retained earnings.

The last two ratios in Table 5-2 illustrate the liquidity of the business. The current ratio is a very common one that is used in bank loans and established as loan covenants. The ratio of current assets to current liabilities should be at least two to one. This ratio simply indicates that the current assets (ie, short-term investments, accounts receivable, and some other assets) versus the current liabilities (ie, accounts payable, accrued liabilities, and the current year's portion of long-term debt) are required in order to reach the level of comfort that, if in fact the loan became stressed, the business would have enough liquidity to cover the debt service.

The final balance is the day's cash balance. This is the amount of cash required, divided by the annual operating expenses, divided by 260 days (ie, the normal number of workdays in a year). As noted in Table 5-2, at least 20 days of cash on hand should be required for an ongoing business's liquidity.

These ratios also contribute to the interpretation of the business and how it has continued to function on a day-to-day basis. Banks are very cognizant of the importance of retained earnings and the maintenance of key ratios and likely will insist on the personal guarantees of the physician-owners, if the practice falls short. Conversely, if the practice is willing to maintain some retained

T A B L E 5-2

Key Credit Indicators and Target Requirements

Category	Computation	Target
Debt service coverage	Net income (after physician compensation) plus interest and depreciation	1.5 times or greater
	Principal and interest payments	
Debt to capitalization	Total debt (including leases)	75% or less
	Total debt plus total equity	
Return on equity	Net income	10% or more
	[(Equity at beginning of year) + (Equity at end of the year)] ÷ 2	
Current ratio	Current assets	2.0:1.0 or better
	Current liabilities	
Days cash balance	Cash	At least 20 days
	(Annual operating expenses ÷ 260 days)*	

* Usual number of workdays per year

earnings and is able to have the kind of liquidity that is illustrated in the targets for these ratios, it is quite likely that the personal guarantees of the physicians will not be necessary.

BENCHMARKING THE MEDICAL PRACTICE

Benchmarks are statistical comparisons that form economic standards upon which to compare and measure the actual performance results of a practice. Benchmarks, therefore, are the methodology to gauge practice performance against independent standards.

Benchmarks, when used within reason, are advantageous as a comparative analysis. In certain instances, benchmarks should be used as primary comparisons against actual performance and, in certain respects, might even be a part of the financial statement comparisons.

Benchmarks are not emphatically correct and, therefore, should be conservatively used—not generating overreaction. They are compiled from various sources with worthy means upon which to base them, but often are unscientific compilations of data.

Benchmarks will vary by different bases. For example, benchmarks will vary by specialty, number of providers, number of locations, geographic region, size of the group, and ownership (eg, hospital-owned, private group). The utilization of benchmarking is an ongoing process that allows the use of an independent standard to compare productivity, expenses, and certain quality measures.

Benchmarking is a way to establish targeted performance and is an excellent tool with which to monitor business/management results. Like most of the methods of financial analysis considered thus far, benchmarking allows for objective, measurable performance standards to be compared against performance as a way to pinpoint trends and receive early warning signals that may be indications of either strength or weakness.

A key point to note is that benchmarking is the use of external sources to compare internal performance. While it is important to measure performance against internal standards, such as the budget and the previous year's performance, it is also beneficial to use external standards. Otherwise, performance that seems beneficial may merely be acceptable. Even if the performance is adequate, it is essential to consider external sources or standards for comparison in pursuit of experience and knowledge of the business. For benchmarking to be credible, the data must be comparative, which is usually the greatest challenge in terms of benchmarking comparisons within the medical practice. For example, when using benchmarking comparisons for productivity within the medical practice, productivity should be comparatively defined, as in comparing "apples to apples."

The following questions illustrate the problems that result when using benchmarking comparisons:

- Is the external source defining productivity as gross charges, net charges, gross or net collections, or a combination of some of these things?
- If it is using gross charges, what about the variances in fee schedules that occur from one practice to another?
- If it is using net charges, what about the variance in contractual allowances?
- What is incorporated within revenue?
- Does revenue include ancillary services that may or may not directly be a part of the professional fees of the practice?

The same problems arise with comparisons with expenses, as cited in the following questions:

- Are the expenses inclusive of any physician benefits or salaries?
- What about employed physicians? Is their expense included in overhead?

These are the basic problems that surface when turning to external sources, which demand close analysis and definition of the external benchmarking sources. Once the definitions are ascertained, numbers usually can be adjusted to reflect somewhat comparable, albeit functional, data upon which to compare and benchmark.

It is essential to define benchmarking comparisons and to use them consistently. Some data for benchmarking is less complex to compare. For example, RVUs used as a measurement standard (ie, a standard in and of itself) are consistently applied once the portion of the RVU (eg, work only versus the entire RVU) is defined.

Other standards for benchmarking comparisons are also more viable when using data, such as the number of FTE employees and costs. It also helps to break the data into smaller components, such as total support staff cost and even data related to accounts receivable (eg, total accounts receivable dollars over a certain number of days, aging).

Productivity Benchmarks

The following are specific productivity benchmarks. Note that many of these benchmarks have similarities to ratios. They include:

- Visits per FTE provider
- RVUs per FTE provider
- Hours worked per provider
- RVUs per visit
- Gross charges per visit
- Net charges per visit

Chapter 8 includes examples of several financial management reports that will elaborate on most of these ratios/benchmarks.

Access

Patient access, of course, is key to the success of any medical practice, starting with the process of appointment scheduling and continuing through the actual visit, with financial success often measured by the length of the appointment and the fees generated. Thus, the following details should be considered when establishing a benchmarking comparison, based upon the access component of the practice:

- Total number of appointment slots per day
- Type of appointment slots
- New patient slots
- Appointment lengths

With these benchmarks, measuring "apples to apples" may be difficult. Although practices differ somewhat, within specialties, they can be quite similar. As an example, the length of appointments in comparison to industry benchmarks should help other physicians understand the expectations. Often, differences are significant between private physicians and those who are employed. In some cases, physicians are employed by hospitals where standards and incentives are not sufficient for maximizing patient visits. The hospital (as a nonpractitioner) has difficulty in influencing behavior because it is hard to put itself in the place of the physician practitioner. One of the advantages of benchmarking is that the industry provides expectations for performance.

Figure 5-1 illustrates the difference between independent and employed physicians in key areas of access.

Based upon the same sources noted in Figure 5-1, the self-employed physician completes 34.4 office hours per week compared to 22.8 office hours per week for the employed physician. The self-employed physician averages 133.1 patient visits per week, while employed physicians see 77.8. Of the self-employed physicians, 75% have weekend hours, versus 54.7% of employed physicians. Finally, 54.5% of the self-employed physicians have evening hours, while 41.5% of employed physicians have evening hours. Benchmarks such as these can provide great insight into practice operations.

FIGURE 5-1

Independent versus Employed Physicians

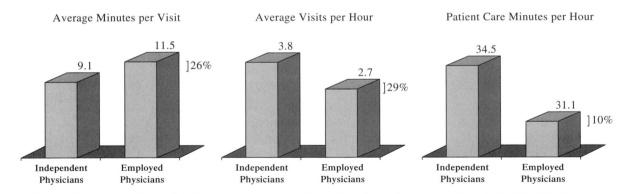

Source: Kikano G, Goodwin MA, Stange KC. Physician employment status and practice patterns. *J Fam Pract.* 1998;46(6):499–505.

Coding and Charge Indicators

A major component of revenue recognition in the medical practice concerns the level of coding that is recorded. Another consideration is the overall fee schedule service mix and RVUs produced. It is beneficial to compare levels of coding to certain standards. Chapter 8 provides a review of specific schedules where a particular practice can plot coding trends and compare these against a typical practice of that specialty. Often with evaluation and management (E/M) codes, the best distribution is thought to be somewhat of a bell curve. That is, there will be fewer occurrences at either end of the E/M codes, with the majority of coding occurring at levels two, three, and four. Although not always the case (nor always the right way), the bell curve can give a basic standard or benchmark from which to manage and monitor performance.

Accounts Receivable Benchmarks

Several key ratios reviewed in this chapter also can be used as benchmarking comparisons. Most sources that compile statistical data provide key accounts receivable indicators, whether as the gross or net collection percentage, aged outstanding in accounts receivable, aged percentage in accounts receivable by 30-day classifications, or other basic data, such as time of service collections or even billing staff ratios to providers. These are all key indicators of accounts receivable data. Moreover, these can be illustrated visually in ways that have a tremendously informative effect on the operation. Figures 5-2, 5-3, and 5-4 illustrate how accounts receivable can be monitored and reviewed on an ongoing basis, through several months of the year, plotting the information all on one graph.

Areas of performance versus industry standards and benchmarks can be monitored within the billing office itself. For example, it is important to measure and consider the number of billing office FTEs per provider. Other billing performance benchmarks include the number of accounts worked per day, patient encounters worked per day, and daily posted payments, all of which are good indicators of the performance of the billing department.

FIGURE 5-2

Accounts Receivable Management Monthly Activity

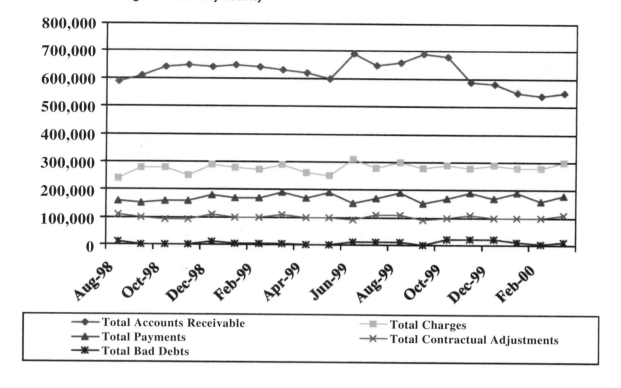

FIGURE 5-3

Days in Accounts Receivable

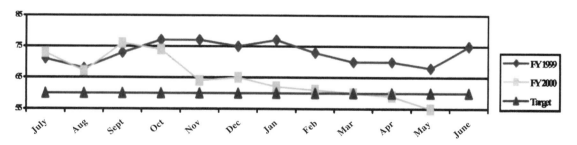

FIGURE 5-4

Accounts Receivable Over 90 Days

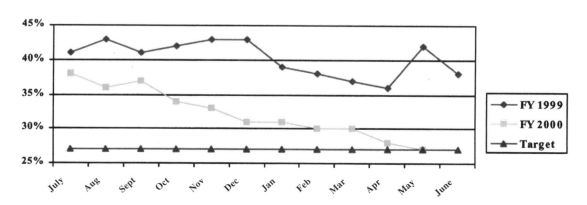

Expense Indicators

Medical practices have many expense indicators, with the greatest expense as personnel. Areas of measurement of personnel cost, which can be benchmarks in comparison to both dollars and the number of staff, should be prominent. Basic benchmark comparisons include the following:

- Staff FTEs to provider
- Staff payroll and benefits or total personnel cost to net charges
- Personnel hours worked per patient visit
- Provider compensation as a percent of revenue and number of visits

Personnel benchmarks are probably the most numerous of all expense costs within the medical practice. Either based upon numbers of FTEs or upon actual dollars, most of the benchmarking sources provide good comparisons to personnel performance. Table 5-3 and Table 5-4 illustrate possible benchmark indicators based upon staffing and how these compare to the actual practice.

Other types of expense should also be considered and compared to standards (eg, medical supplies, laboratory supplies, facility expense, malpractice expense, marketing, G&A cost). It is also important to break down expenses by providers versus nonproviders. Most benchmarks provide their overhead totals based upon cost prior to consideration of any provider expense. This is typically called above the line in that all expenses are considered prior to the cost of the actual providers (whether they are owners or not). Other expenses not common to overhead, such as interest, depreciation, and other non-cash items, might also be separated from the ongoing operating expenses, but nonetheless, are a central component of the overhead.

Performance Indicators

Day-to-day operations can also be compared with certain standards, which may include operational matters, such as:

- Amount of wait time per visit
- Wait time on the telephone
- Access wait time by appointment type
- Number of no-shows
- Transcription turnaround
- Accounts worked per collector FTE per day
- Words or lines transcribed per day
- Authorization turnaround time
- Return telephone call wait time

Many, but not all, of these indicators are readily available for benchmarks. Moreover, several consulting firms tabulate this information and develop standards based upon their clients' expenses, as well as their own knowledge of what are appropriate standards.

TABLE 5-3

All Affiliated Medical Groups Summary of FTEs

	Medical Group "A" FTEs	Medical Group "B" FTEs	Total FTEs	FTEs per Provider*	Benchmark
Reception/ Clerical	104.00	106.0	210.00	1.05	1.10
Clinical	70.00	60.00	130.00	0.65	0.75
Management and Other	34.00	30.00	64.00	0.32	0.50
Total FTEs	**208.00**	**196.00**	**404.00**	**2.02**	**2.35**

* Assume a total of 200 providers (FTEs) in the practice

TABLE 5-4

Summary of FTEs by Medical Group Practice

	Medical Group "A" FTEs per Provider*	Medical Group "B" FTEs per Provider*	Benchmark
Reception/Clerical	1.04	1.06	1.10
Clinical	0.70	0.60	0.75
Management and Other	0.34	0.30	0.50
Total FTEs	**2.08**	**1.96**	**2.35**

* Assume each group has 100 FTE providers

It is important to monitor revenue, expenses, and other operational performance measures in comparison to benchmark standards. Although this requires a greater amount of data collection, it is well worth it to compare your practice operations with such definitive comparisons.

In addition, the use of benchmarking negates the perspective that this practice is different from everybody else's and, therefore, whatever performance results exist are essentially what has to take place (nothing should change). This flawed thinking can change when comparing industry standards to performance. The attitude of "we don't need to change," or "we have the right formula to fit our practice," can be influenced through the type of hard and comparative data that benchmarks provide. Implementing changes in the practice can be difficult, especially when politics, as well as egos, get in the way. Benchmark data that is reliable, comparable, and compiled throughout many years, can influence change and provide a credible mechanism for accountability.

Benchmarks are invaluable tools and important to the successful financial management of the practice. They can influence behavior transformations when nothing else can convince those in the practice to change. Benchmarking is most effective when integrated into day-to-day operations, which usually comes from processing the data, ensuring that it is comparable, and then developing a well-organized system of management reports (including visuals, such as graphs, charts, tables, and so on) that translate the data into an understandable format.

Benchmarking Sources

Benchmarking data, as used in these examples, is available through a number of sources, such as the following:

- American Medical Association
- American Medical Group Association
- Center for Healthcare Industry Performance Studies
- Medical Economics
- Medical Group Management Association
- Practice Support Resources, Inc.
- Individual research initiatives via consulting firms

Whatever the source of the benchmarks, it is essential to understand the data. It should be accompanied by a thorough explanation of how the data was compiled and of what the data consists.

SUMMARY

Ratios and benchmarks, which are two important, albeit essential, tools to beneficial financial management of the medical practice, were covered in some detail in this chapter. Interrelated as they are, ratios and benchmarks should be used on a regular basis, perhaps as often as weekly or daily. There are several prerequisites to ensure success in the accumulation of data. They are as follows:

- The information should be accurately compiled
- Outside information should be provided by accurate and sufficient resources
- The information should be used as a tool for learning and enabling change
- The organization should be committed to the use of the data
- Staff should be trained on how to use the data
- Ratio and benchmark data should be succinctly presented

With these tools in hand, the practice of using ratios and benchmarks can be perhaps the single greatest tool for implementing change that ultimately engenders success within the practice.

Internal Controls and Safeguards

This chapter addresses key elements of internal cash management controls and safeguarding of practice assets. Practices must ensure that cash is carefully handled and deposited into the practice's bank account, even though the amounts may not be substantial. The effective control and management of incoming monies and outgoing disbursements is more important than ever, based upon the current need for maximizing cash flow in the practice.

CASH FLOW MANAGEMENT

Using cash effectively is essential to successful medical practice operations, yet it often presents many challenges. Frequently, practices must do more work with fewer employees, which decreases the likelihood of adequate internal controls. Too few employees handling cash without guidelines leads to less efficient cash management and greater risk of latent fraudulent activities.

Cash flow management has two initiatives of equal importance: (1) to maximize collections and (2) to maintain internal controls. Although the attention to each should be the same, some internal controls may be forfeited in an effort to maximize collections. With the physician-owner assuming a more active role and supervision of certain processes within the practice, some lapses in internal controls can be minimized. These two aspects—collections and controls— should be weighed in the balance of other demands on time, knowledge of the personnel, level of trust, and structure of the organization.

Banking Relationships and Bank Accounts

Generally, medical practices should establish and use a minimum of two bank accounts. They include the following:

■ **Regular operating account.** This account should be used for most of the regular disbursements of accounts payable and payroll. Only enough money should be maintained in this account to avert usage charges, plus an additional cushion to cover incidental checks that are written throughout the month. Monies for paying the monthly accounts payable and for meeting payroll should be transferred from an investment or sweep account into the regular operating account to cover the disbursements.

In some cases, larger practices may be justified in setting up a separate payroll account to isolate payroll disbursements from general operating expenses. A payroll account is usually established as a zero balance account. This simply means that only enough monies to cover the payroll and related payroll taxes are transferred into the account at the time of disbursement. No excess monies are maintained in this account; thus, the term *zero balance.*

■ **Money market or investment/sweep account.** Most practices are able to generate some excess cash flow, at least on an interim basis. In this event, a system should be established for the bank to automatically transfer (or sweep) balances in the operating account to an investment account. Investment accounts generally do not bear substantial amounts of interest, although the yield is likely to be higher than most operating accounts. At a minimum, isolating excess monies for the purpose of earning some additional interest is preferable than allowing it to remain stagnant.

Managing Incoming Cash

The following are points to remember in the operation and management of incoming cash:

■ Deposits should be made on a regular basis, preferably daily, unless the amounts are so small they do not warrant the effort. A separate deposit should be made for each day's receipts, even if the deposit is not physically taken to the bank each day. The total dollars deposited should balance with the summary activity from the practice management information system's close out for each day to verify that all funds received on a day were in fact deposited.

■ Insurance and explanation of benefits statements should be reviewed and balanced against the accompanying payments.

■ Checks received should be logged in, designated by payer, with date of receipt and the amount. A daily collection summary worksheet (see Table 6-1) should be maintained and balanced against these totals.

■ Each payment from an individual payer should be separately listed on the deposit slip to serve as an audit trail and as proper documentation for posting the receivable. Often, this information can be posted using practice management software. The accompanying reports, generated from the software program, provide the documentation.

■ Itemize large checks from a single payer that are reimbursing several charges to ensure that they concur with the billing statements.

■ Denials should be tracked and reasons for nonreceipt of these monies documented, then researched, and resubmitted.

Cash management is a daily occurrence. For the benefit of the physicians, cash flow should be managed each day, using a simple cash flow tracking sheet formula:

TABLE 6-1

Daily Collections Summary Worksheet

Date: _____

Check No.	Description/Patient Name	Physician	Cash	Credit Check	Card	Total	Payment Received

Beginning balance + deposits − disbursements = ending balance

This formula can be used on a daily, weekly, monthly, and yearly basis, but should be used at least weekly. This analysis can be reconciled to the bank statement and financial book balance each month to be certain of an accurate daily *cash flash report*.

Much of the value of beneficial financial management of a medical practice centers on the manager's ability to look at trends in an effort to anticipate cash flow results. History tells a lot, particularly about a practice that has been in existence for some time. Often, the history of cash flow within certain reciprocal periods will be replicated in similar periods in the future. All of these reports should be tools that enable the practice manager to manage cash flow and anticipate future requirements.

With the right information, the physician-owner can anticipate cash needs for the future and will not overdistribute monies that will be needed for future disbursements. For example, if a particular practice and its physician-owners have $50,000 in excess funds at the end of a given month, they may be tempted to disburse all or most of those monies, perceiving this as true profit. However, if, for example, a large disbursement, such as an annual malpractice premium is due in the following month or even within the next two to three months, sufficient monies for the premiums should be retained to pay for the amount due rather than disbursed as profit.

A competent cash manager can manage cash and anticipate the inflow and outflow, based upon regular analysis, regular and reliable reports, and the history of comparable periods, to make appropriate decisions in this regard.

Another important aspect of proper cash management is paying bills on a timely basis. Most invoices are sent with a date designating when the payment is due, usually within 30 days. If a practice receives an invoice that is not due for 20 days, it should not be paid until near the end of that period, unless the creditor/supplier offers a discount for early payment. This should be assessed as the invoice is received, approved, and processed for payment.

Part of cash management in any medical practice is ascertaining the need for borrowing money. As it relates to working capital, practices will often have reciprocal trends in their cash flow. In other words, at certain times, they may lack enough cash flow to pay all the bills. However, in time, corrections will occur due to reciprocal peaks and valleys of operations. For example, a pediatric practice will typically have its busy season after the first of the year, which translates to greater receipts soon after. In many instances, a practice needs a working capital line of credit that is utilized with care—not as a long-term loan—that will not be repaid within a 12-month period. Routinely, most banks will require that a working capital loan be completely repaid for at least a 30-day period within that 12-month time frame.

Petty Cash

A petty cash fund, usually about $100, is a small source of cash to pay amounts that are usually impractical to pay by check. Every practice should maintain such a fund. Accompanying each petty cash disbursement should be a form plus a copy of the receipt or invoice pertaining to that disbursement. The responsibility for the fund should be vested in the practice administrator, managing physician, or for a larger practice, the financial manager/bookkeeper.

Petty cash should not be a major factor within the medical practice's cash flow management. Management of petty cash does not involve a lot of money and potential losses are low; however, the fund does need to be monitored, with adherence to policies and procedures that are instituted. The petty cash fund should be periodically reconciled and items listed as disbursements should be justified. (See Table 6-2.)

Key Policies Pertaining to Petty Cash

The following are key points to keep in mind regarding petty cash:

- The practice administrator or appointed physician should approve all disbursements from petty cash.
- The petty cash fund should be counted and balanced (if feasible, by any staff member other than the petty cash custodian) at the time of reimbursement of the fund.
- Personal checks of the staff members should never be paid out of the petty cash fund, nor should IOUs be placed in the petty cash fund.

TABLE 6-2

Petty Cash Reconciliation Form

Disbursements

Date Starting:_____ (A) Starting Balance $_____

No.	Date	Item Purchased	(B) Amount	(C) Balance
		Total		

Total Transactions: (A) — (B) = (C)

$_____ $_____ $_____

Request for Reimbursement: $_____

Submitted By:Date:_____ Date_____

- At regular intervals, a check to Petty Cash should be written for the sum of Received of Petty Cash forms and receipts. This documentation should be stapled to the Petty Cash Reconciliation Form for verification.

In summary, petty cash should be maintained as a mechanism for minor disbursements within the practice's operations. The petty cash fund should be designated only for very minor items, mainly for convenience. Payments made by checks are the preferable means for paying expenses in order to develop the proper paper trails and to follow protocols.

INTERNAL CONTROL ISSUES FOR THE MEDICAL PRACTICE

Routine transactions involving cash receipts within a typical medical practice include:

- Cash and checks received through the mail (eg, from patients, insurance companies, managed care organizations, third-party administrators, Medicare, Medicaid, miscellaneous receipts)
- Over-the-counter receipts from patients paid at the time of visit (eg, co-pays, deductibles)
- Over-the-counter collections on accounts from patients
- Monies credited to the practice's bank account for payments received from bank cards and other charge cards, including Visa, MasterCard, Discover, American Express, and others

Internal controls over cash can be described as a combination of policies and procedures that are established and maintained, accompanied by sufficient auditing and review to ensure that checks and balances are in place and maintained. The fundamental concept of internal controls is separation of duties. That is, the individual who receives the cash, the one who posts the amount received to the books of record, and the one who deposits the money in the bank are not the same person.

Moreover, internal controls involve a quick daily review of certain important balancing totals by the practice manager and, on occasion, by the physician. In the case of a small practice, the physician must review the daily total because typically the practice administrator performs most of the cash handling functions; separation of duties is not possible because of the size of the staff. The physician must assume responsibility for regularly reviewing reports pertaining to cash.

An internal control system must be tailored to the individual practice, adapting textbook theory to a practical, realistic, and economical approach to assignments and responsibilities. Practices should consult an outside accountant or Certified Public Accountant (CPA) who is familiar with the practice for advice on establishing appropriate internal controls. Using an outside accountant or CPA for certain functions on a monthly basis will, in fact, enhance internal controls that might otherwise be lacking in the small practice. For example, the outside accountant who reconciles the bank accounts will likely have access to all receipts and disbursements that are processed through those accounts, especially the main operating account. The apt accountant should look for things that are inappropriate and question items for their authenticity when issues arise.

In all, medical practices greatly need to implement internal controls for all aspects of cash management. The suspicion of fraud within the practice does not engender trust or loyalty among the staff members. Nevertheless, staff should understand the importance of internal controls and the need for other checks and balances, such as the use of the outside accounting professional. Often, the lapses that occur are not due to intentional fraudulent activities; they are a result of innocent mistakes or careless errors. For this reason, policies and procedures must be in place and followed at all times to guard against errors and intentional fraudulent acts.

Rarely, if ever, should exceptions be made to a practice's internal control guidelines. Policies and procedures of this nature are not needed if they are not followed.

The following are general recommendations for controlling cash and maintaining good internal controls:

■ The staff member opening the mail records all payments received through the mail in a Mail Receipts Journal (see Table 6-3) before transferring the payments to the staff member who is making the deposit. The Journal includes a section for itemizing payments that are not directly related to patient accounts (eg, fees for depositions, copies of records to insurance companies). Periodically, the practice administrator reconciles these records with the actual deposit slip.

■ Cash paid to physicians for services not connected with the practice (eg, honoraria, rental income, interest income, any other nonphysician professionally generated fees) should not be included in the practice deposits. These monies should go directly to the physician, who in turn maintains a log to track these payments as they are received. Any income not related to patients' fees (eg, copies of medical records) that are deposited into the practice operating account, must be posted to the daily journal to reconcile charges and receipts and to prevent overstatement of the collection rate at month- and year-end.

- Procedures for handling cash should be clearly defined and responsibilities specifically assigned, not left to the first staff member who can get to it each day. Rotate these job functions on a periodic basis.

- The functions of cash collections and cash disbursements should each be assigned to staff members (ie, the same staff member should not handle collections [accounts receivable] and disbursements [accounts payable]).

- The handling of cash should be totally separate from records maintenance. The employee opening the mail, counting the receipts, and making the daily deposit should not be posting those receipts against the accounts receivable.

- Someone who does not handle the cash or maintain the accounting records, preferably an outside accountant or CPA who regularly prepares financial statements for the practice, should complete all bank account reconciliation. All staff members, including the practice administrator, should be answerable to someone—even if it is to an outside consultant—to establish accountability.

TABLE 6-3

Mail Receipts Journal

Mail Receipts Journal *Receipts of January 20, 20__*

Check/Reference Number, etc.	Source	Sender	City/State	Amount
560060	Check	Cigna Health Plan/HMO	Atlanta, GA	$5,630.00
19060	Check	Group Resources, Inc./TPA	Norcross, GA	460.00
220460	Check	Great-West Insurance Co.	Atlanta, GA	860.00
335	Check	Kay Arthur	Alpharetta, GA	100.00
1.00890	Check	U.S. Govt/Medicare	Atlanta, GA	1,550.00
Other Income 220471	Check	Blue Cross/GA – deposition fee	Atlanta, GA	500.00
Total				$9,100.00

Explanation of Headings:

Check/Reference Number: Patient or other payer's pre-numbered check or other voucher number on payment advice.

Source: Type of payment, such as cash, check, draft, bank credit, credit card. (Typically, these will be assigned a number in a computerized journal system.)

Sender: Name of patient and/or other payer, including insurance company, governmental institution, managed care administrator, etc. (Use assigned number system for a computerized journal.)

- All employees involved in the handling of cash for the accounting records must take periodic vacations. During this absence, another staff member should handle those functions. Periodic, unannounced shifts in job responsibilities should occur to expose or possibly prevent collusion.

- All employees handling cash or accounting records should be bonded. The need for this varies with the size of the practice and individual situation. Consider purchasing office overhead (ie, employee dishonesty) insurance, if economically feasible.

- Statements mailed to patients or other payers must be prepared and mailed by a staff member other than the cashier. Include instructions on the statement about whom to call in case of questions. If the person who makes the deposits also does the billing, an opportunity is provided to cover up, misapply, and reallocate funds.

- Cash payments received on the day of treatment should be charged to the accounts receivable ledger and simultaneously credited. Otherwise, dishonest employees may use opportunities such as this for theft. The actual day of service payments, some of which may be in cash, are more easily stolen and covered up (ie, via unethical record keeping) if controls are not in place.

- At the end of each day, patient encounter forms and receipts should be collected and reconciled with the over-the-counter cash receipts.

  - A pre-numbered duplicate receipt should be filled out with one copy given to the patient for over-the-counter cash payments on account (not at the time of service).

  - Encounter forms should be pre-numbered and prepared for each patient expected on a given day. Walk-in patients should be issued an encounter form in the proper numerical sequence to those issued for scheduled patients.

  - At the end of each day, all encounter forms should be collected and placed in numerical sequence. Include forms that were issued for no-shows. Account for all forms. Do not destroy unused encounter forms.

  - Over-the-counter collections (eg, cash, check, credit card payments) should be totaled separately from mailed receipts. Attach the calculator tape to the batch of encounter forms and receipts and give them to the practice administrator. The total payment shown on the encounter forms and receipts should equal the total of the over-the-counter receipts for that day.

  - Accounts receivable posting may be done at the time of service or at the end of the day when all encounter forms and receipts are collected.

Fraud and Dishonesty

Embezzlement of assets, also known as misappropriation of funds, is a frequent problem in a medical practice, posing a significant threat to the practice's resources and ongoing viability. Fraud is usually the result of the lack of internal controls or a lack of adherence to basic policies and procedures that are established.

Asset misappropriation occurs in businesses as either theft of cash or inventory and all other assets. The primary risk to medical practices is the loss of cash (or receivables that have not yet turned into cash) through dishonest employees. Practices with numerous locations or branches and those that stand as individual entities are equally vulnerable to theft through embezzlement and other misappropriations by employees.

Figure 6-1 uses a tree to illustrate how fraud is committed within an organization. The two branches to the trunk illustrate the prominence of misappropriation of cash over other assets in the course of employee theft and embezzlement. In an article in the *Journal of Accountancy,* reports from a study indicate that in 2,608

FIGURE 6-1

Fraud and Dishonesty Within an Organization

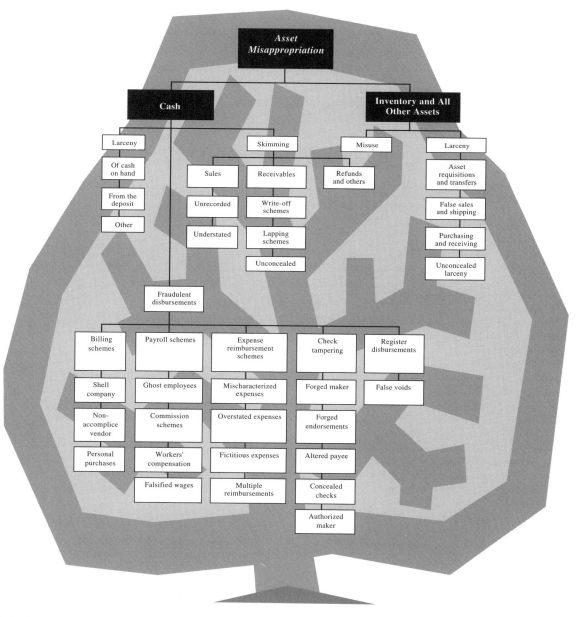

Source: Wells JT. Enemies within. *Journal of Accountancy.* December 2001.

cases of occupational fraud and abuse, nearly nine in ten illegal schemes involved misappropriation of cash.

Figure 6-1 illustrates that cash is a major source of asset misappropriation, largely through various facets of larceny and skimming of incoming cash. The fraudulent disbursement of outgoing cash, however, can follow many paths. Table 6-4 illustrates the early warning signs of cash misappropriation.

More specific ways that funds are misappropriated in the medical practice are listed here.

Mail receipts:

- **Lapping.** Diverting practice funds and reporting them at some time after collection. Usually funds received from one account are credited against another one from which cash has previously been diverted.

- **Temporarily Using Practice Funds.** Borrowing without falsifying records. Cash is diverted for personal use with the intention of paying it back later. The payback may or may not occur. Chances are, if the employee thinks he or she has gotten away with it, he or she will justify or rationalize not replacing the money.

- **Bad Debt Improperly Charged Off.** Charging off a patient's account balance and pocketing the cash from a payment. (All write-offs must have a supervisor's approval before posting. The physician and/or outside consultant should also initial the write-offs.)

TABLE 6-4

Early Warning Signs of Cash Misappropriation

The three principle methods that employees use to misappropriate cash can show up early in an organization's books. CPAs should be alert to simple trends when determining a company's risk of material embezzlement. Consider one or more of the following:

Skimming:

- Decreasing cash to total current assets
- A decreasing ratio of cash to credit card sales
- Flat or declining sales with increasing cost of sales
- Increasing accounts receivable compared with cash
- Delayed posting of accounts receivable payments

Larceny:

- Unexplained cash discrepancies
- Altered or forged deposit slips
- Customer billing and payment complaints
- Rising in transit deposits during bank reconciliations

Fraudulent Disbursements:

- Increasing soft expenses (eg, consulting, advertising)
- Employee home address matches a vendor's address
- Vendor address is a post office box or mail drop
- Vendor name consists of initials or vague business purpose (Employees often use their own initials when setting up dummy companies (eg, JTW Enterprises.)
- Excessive voided, missing, or destroyed checks

Source: Wells JT. Enemies within. *Journal of Accountancy.* December 2001.

- **Excluding Miscellaneous Income.** Diverting monies by not reporting small amounts that were received (eg, payment for deposition fees, fees for copies of records).

Over-the-counter transactions:

- Fraud occurs when an employee fails to report (and keeps) all proceeds from cash received from patients who paid in person.
- Fraud occurs when a smaller fee is posted rather than the true amount of the charge.

What are the reasons for fraud? Embezzlement or fraudulent activity is often not committed because employees are inherently dishonest or have planned to do this from the beginning of their employment. Mostly, an employee commits fraud when he or she is experiencing external economic pressures or perceives that he or she has not been dealt with fairly (eg, has not received a due raise). In other cases, an employee is faced with a temptation that he or she cannot withstand. These are the logical reasons why fraud occurs. For an explicit understanding of how the stage is set for fraudulent activities, consider the following:

- Internal controls are poor or do not exist:
  - Controls are stated but not enforced; lapses are allowed to occur
  - Offenders go unpunished
  - Examples of high ethical conduct are not set
- Individual employees have significant, personal financial pressures due to:
  - Personal indebtedness
  - Lifestyle behavior (eg, excessive drinking, gambling, drug use)
  - Extravagant living standards
- Employees believe they have been mistreated:
  - Low or no salary increases have been given
  - Benefits have been reduced (eg, increase in health insurance premiums)
- Employees believe physicians are greedy and that they do not share profits with the employees
- Employees hold the attitude that "they'll never miss it"

FINANCIAL SAFEGUARDS

The following sections present several key points that warrant regular review and consideration by the medical practice. The first section is a series of questions that relate to financial safeguards and controls and whether these are in place within the practice.

Deterring Embezzlement Activity

These are questions that should be asked and answered on a regular basis. Periodically, the practice should undergo an external or, if large enough, internal audit process to ensure that the following controls are in place:

- To what extent is segregation of duties possible?
- To what extent are supervisory controls possible?
- To what extent is an internal audit practical?
- Does the practice need to have an external audit along with implemented internal controls?
- Is it practical for employees to be bonded? Can background checks on employees be completed prior to hiring?
- Can supervisory controls be implemented to ensure strong internal controls and financial safeguards? For example, is there a policy to control the use of prenumbered checks and to make sure that all checks are accounted for?
- Who performs the bank reconciliation?
- Who reviews the bank reconciliation?
- Who approves write-offs and contractual adjustments?
- Is there staff cross-training in place?
- Who reviews supporting documentation for disbursements?
- Who validates whether vendors are legitimate by confirming that they exist and have a viable business?

Several additional ways to reduce the risk of fraudulent activities and to prevent embezzlement of practice funds are illustrated in the following recommendations:

1. Set up written control procedures and make sure that the employees follow them.
2. Avoid allowing one employee to have complete control over the entire sequence of cash transactions.
3. Limit access of cash to specified employees.
4. Make sure employees who do not handle receipts or cash disbursements maintain the accounting records.
5. If segregation of duties is impractical, make sure all work is periodically reviewed.
6. Have outside accountants perform periodic test checks and auditing reviews.
7. Regularly review contractual assignments, daily activity reports, and appointment calendars.
8. Periodically follow a random sampling of patients through the office from the charge ticket and the day sheet to the bank deposit.
9. Make sure that all bank accounts are balanced monthly.
10. Use prenumbered checks and superbills.
11. Keep records of all cash receipts and deposit them daily. Do not make payments out of undeposited receipts.
12. Compare cash receipts that are posted in the (computerized) system to the cash actually deposited in the bank.
13. Keep tight controls over petty cash. Make cash payments by check whenever possible.
14. Make sure the employee who signs checks is not the same employee who makes bank deposits, and that the check signer

has the opportunity to review supporting documentation (ie, invoices).

15. Stamp checks *For Deposit Only* when they are received.

16. Require employees to take vacations. (Embezzlers are often caught when they are not around to cover their tracks.)

17. Provide adequate instructions to patients regarding the proper mailing of check remittances. Be sure to inform the patient that checks are to be made payable to the practice, not an individual or a physician.

18. Require employees to provide a written receipt to patients who make over-the-counter payment for services rendered on a different day. If a rubber stamp is used in the *pay to the order of* portion of the check, require that it be stamped in the presence of the patient who is paying. Ask patients to fill out the line on the check indicating for what the payment is being made. Consider posting these instructions at the front desk.

19. Consider purchasing bonding insurance for employees.

20. Promptly follow up on past due accounts.

Finally, early warning signs to detect fraud are available if time is made for observation. Here are some additional early warning signals:

1. The employee who never takes vacations.
2. The employee who insists on doing everything himself/herself.
3. The employee who is obviously living beyond his/her means.
4. The employee who complains, "We do all the work, and they get all the money!"
5. Two employees with access to receipts who frequently arrange to make deposits together (ie, the employee who opens the mail and the one who prepares the bank deposit).
6. The employee who is openly critical of the practice and, in particular, its physicians or owners.

SUMMARY

Strong internal controls and safeguarding of assets involves constancy, purpose, and following of established policies and procedures. The first order of business is to put internal checks and balances in place. The cash handling functions of one employee and those of another will be different for each practice. Regardless of the distribution of tasks, internal controls will be fortified with adequate policies and some checks and balances in place (eg, individuals who are checking behind other individuals, including outside parties, such as the practice's accountant).

The other major component of proper internal controls and safeguarding of assets within the practice is fraud prevention. The best way of dealing with fraud is to prevent it from ever happening by removing its temptation. To safeguard against fraud, the practice should conduct periodic audits. Become acquainted with the *fraud tree* as illustrated in Figure 6-1. In particular, look for areas that are most vulnerable within the medical practice, such as areas involving day-to-day handling of cash and processing payments. Detect fraud by segregating duties, having checks and balances in place, and conducting surprise audits.

Finally, watch for the general behavior of employees and, to some extent, be aware of personal matters that are going on in their lives. If such checks and balances are not in place, honest employees may be vulnerable to temptation when under severe financial stress. Also, look for employees who, on occasion, believe they have been dealt with unfairly. They may rationalize their mistreatment as justification for theft. Sometimes employees assume that "the practice will never miss it." A close watch for these behaviors will safeguard against loss of funds that the practice has earned and needs.

Monitoring cash management and maintaining internal controls is a constant undertaking that should never be neglected, even for one day. Sound cash planning forms the backbone for an efficiently operated medical practice. Physicians may deliver the highest quality care services and generate substantial revenue; however, if the funds are not collected, properly placed in the operating account, and prudently managed, the practice will not be successful. The productivity of the providers makes little difference in practice performance if the funds that are brought in are misappropriated.

chapter 7

Budgeting and Pro Formas

This chapter focuses on the process of budgeting and forecasting performance, and covers many aspects of preparation and planning that are used as an ongoing measurement of performance. The chapter also addresses the preparation and use of pro formas to project income and expenses for the purpose of planning new initiatives for the health care entity.

BUDGETING

A budget process is the foundation for all financial activities of the medical practice. *Budgeting* includes the coordination, control, and reporting of variances between budgeted and actual results. The budget provides and coordinates controls that are needed to effectively manage the practice and relates to all of the policies and procedures needed to accomplish a practice's objectives.

Budgeting has long been used by businesses in all industries. Traditionally, the medical practice has been financially successful without such a tool. However, because cost control and other fiscal pressures have developed, it is now necessary for a medical practice to budget like other businesses.

Why Use a Budget?

The managing physician and the practice administrator should understand how to forecast revenues and budget expenses. Practices that have the financial expertise may do budgeting internally, although it is acceptable to engage outside assistance from an accounting professional.

A budget is generally prepared for a short period (ie, compared to long-range and strategic plans) and is expressed in basic financial terminology. It should be simple enough for the non-accounting professional to understand and use. Simply stated, a budget measures actual financial performance against standards. A parallel example is to set a personal or professional goal and direct all activities to reach it.

From a practical standpoint, a budget provides an excellent means for understanding the productivity and expense levels that are required to keep the practice financially healthy. Practice administrators that participate in the budget planning exercise professionally benefit by adding a new dimension to their skills. By monitoring the actual results versus the budget throughout the year, the practice administrator becomes aware of trends that facilitate better control of future costs. Preparing and monitoring a budget throughout the year (ie, actual performance versus budgeting standards), provides early warning signs of negative trends within the practice.

Budgeting is as much a cognitive process as an accounting one. The physician(s) and staff must seriously reflect upon changes in the health care industry and how those changes relate to the practice. Plans for expansion, operational changes concerning services and payer mix, and the physicians' future goals and plans must be considered in the process.

Budgeting Functions and Accomplishments

To summarize, a budget accomplishes the following:

- Provides an accurate, timely tool to review anticipated versus actual results
- Helps control current performance
- Helps predict future performance and anticipated problem areas
- Determines where resources should be allocated
- Provides an early warning device of budget variations
- Highlights early signs of future opportunities
- Provides the physician(s), office personnel, and practice administrator a practice management tool
- Provides a concise financial summary in an understandable format

THE TOTAL MANAGEMENT SYSTEM

Budgeting entails the analysis of all operational and management functions within the practice. It requires *planning* and *action,* followed by constant *review* and *control* considerations. Budgeting involves the following activities:

- Determining the initial strategy
- Developing plans to carry out the strategy
- Reflecting the strategic goals and planning process
- Coordinating the organizational structure to fit the goals and strategic plan
- Designing maximization of productivity and revenue
- Developing accurate reporting systems
- Developing management control systems with the ability to react and respond to variances

The budgeting process is a small, but very important, link in the financial management cycle chain. For the financial cycle to work well, none of its components (ie, links in the chain) can be broken. This is also especially pertinent to the revenue cycle. Budgeting, forecasting, and cost allocation are vital to a healthy, successful management system.

THE BUDGETING PROCESS

The budgeting process begins with the gathering of information prior to the meeting to be used as resource material for forming the initial budget. The following is a list of appropriate resource materials to be collected:

- Year-end financial statements for the prior three fiscal periods, preferably broken down by month or, at the very least, by quarter. Depending on the legal structure of the practice, tax returns may also be beneficial.

- All legal documents supporting contractual agreements, including real estate leases, equipment leases, contracts for cleaning maintenance, landscaping, and so on.

- List of major equipment purchases anticipated for the coming year, including the estimated cost and suggested method of payment for each. Consider all possible acquisitions, regardless of the cost effect on the practice (ie, a wish list of items).

- Fee schedules.

Once this information has been collected, plan on holding an extended session, or sessions, to incorporate the necessary analysis and to discuss processes.

Who Should Be Involved?

The budgeting process starts with a budget planning session. All key decision-makers and other personnel in cost containment roles must attend. Those participating should include:

- Physician(s)
- Practice administrator
- Department heads, if applicable

What Information Is Needed?

The budget is derived from information available through a variety of sources, such as the following:

- Year-end financial statements for the prior three fiscal periods, preferably broken down by month or, at the very least, by quarter. Depending on the legal structure of the practice, tax returns may also be beneficial.

- All legal documents supporting contractual agreements. These include real estate leases, equipment leases, contracts for cleaning, maintenance, landscaping, etc.

- List of major equipment purchases anticipated for the coming year, including the estimated cost and suggested method of payment for each. Consider all possible acquisitions, regardless of the cost impact on the practice (ie, a wish list of items).

- Fee schedules.

- All productivity reports or practice analysis that are generated by the practice management software system. These include analysis by physician of overall production versus collections, payer mix, utilization information, and so on.

■ A list of planned new services for the coming year. In consultation with the physician(s), this should be determined and incorporated into the budgeting process.

■ List of outside influences that may directly affect the practice (eg, specific industry issues, managed care contracting changes, political issues, demographic considerations, technological matters, general business considerations).

Outside Influences on the Budgeting Process

The medical practice has been somewhat insulated from the phenomenon of outside influences on the budgeting process. As changes occur in the environment of governmental agencies and private outside payers (ie, insurance companies), the influence of the outside world on a medical practice increases. Hence, the following economic factors must be considered in the budgeting process:

■ Inflation rates

■ Anticipated interest or cost of capital rates

■ Labor cost

■ Regulatory influences and requirements

■ Material and supply costs, including office and medical supplies

■ Competition considerations that directly affect the practice

■ Demographic considerations, including possible changes

■ Products and services being offered within the practice

■ Potential changes to other health care providers that will affect the practice (eg, hospital or practice mergers, HMO acquisitions, divestitures)

How to Begin the Budgeting Process

Budgeting is an activity that consists of many steps. The following information will help the participants to systematically complete the process using a budget planning worksheet.

Major Components of the Budget Planning Worksheet
The Budget Planning Worksheet is a critical tool in the budget planning process. In order to efficiently use the Budget Planning Worksheet, the administrator must have a clear understanding of the major types of revenue and expenses. They are as follows:

■ **Gross revenue.** Gross revenue refers to all production that is placed on the books by the physician for services rendered. This includes such items as office visits, consultations, hospital visits and procedures, ancillary procedures, nursing home work, and outpatient procedures.

■ **Contractual adjustments to revenue.** The adjustment is the resulting discount applied to gross revenue (eg, generated from

Medicare and Medicaid price reductions and managed care discounts on both a fee-for-service and a capitated basis).

■ **Fee-for-service revenue.** The revenue produced for the physician as a result of the specific service performed. No consideration is made for number of patients seen or any other outside influence other than actually considering the fee to be charged for that specific service (normally this fee is discounted from the practice's standard fee schedule).

■ **Capitated income.** Income tied to a number of *covered lives* that are subject to a managed care contract in which a guaranteed payment rate per covered life is paid to the physician, regardless of whether the patient, subject to the contract, is seen by the physician.

■ **Net collections.** Because most practices are accounted for on a *cash basis*, this is the actual revenue referred to for the budget planning process. It represents the actual receipts of the practice, net of all contractual agreements, and is a result of the actual collections of accounts receivable from all sources of professional services that are performed by the physician. The net collections total, therefore, is the most critical item of the revenue side of the budget planning process upon which decisions are to be based.

■ **Fixed expenses.** These are the expenses that are not affected by patient volume. Examples are rent, salaries (excluding commissions), interest payments on fixed debt, insurance, property taxes, and utilities.

■ **Variable expenses.** These are expenses that change in direct proportion to the number of patients seen. Examples are medical supplies, office supplies, laboratory costs, medications, and interest on an operating working capital line of credit.

■ **Period expenses.** Costs incurred over time as opposed to a level of activity. As an example, salaries are quoted as an annual amount, but paid over a period of time during the year.

Developing the Budget Planning Worksheet

The Budget Planning Worksheet provides a basis to formulate the financially compiled information. The following is a brief review of the key contents of this simple worksheet (see Table 7-1):

■ **Items.** These represent typical revenue and expense accounts to be considered in the budgeting process. While there is no all-inclusive list, those listed in Table 7-1 and Table 7-2 are typical practice revenue and expense accounts. The list should be prepared to fit the needs of the practice. For the Budget Planning Worksheet, revenue represents net collections from the practice. For purposes of this exercise, do not include gross production in revenues prior to contractual adjustments and/or discounts. Rather, net collections represent the final, anticipated collections total, net of all such contractual adjustments and discounts.

Expense items include broad accounts, such as accounting, contributions, insurance, supplies, rent, salaries, taxes, depreciation, and similar expenses. Again, these items should be specific to the needs of the practice.

- **1999–2000 columns.** The 1999 and 2000 columns in Table 7-1 and Table 7-2 represent the previous two years (assuming this is a 2002 budget). These are the actual operating results for each of the items listed for these years.

- **Percent change.** The percentage change is the difference between 2000 and 1999 actual results, calculated as a percentage. The computation is similar to the one previously noted in the first Percentage Change column.

- **Initial budget.** This amount is the first item entered on the worksheet for projected totals. Its input is without the benefit of detailed analysis and consideration on the part of the physician(s) and practice administrator. In other words, it is the initial pass at the numbers based upon prior year's results.

- **Final budget.** The totals in the Final Budget are the result of much deliberation, analyses, and consideration of the numbers. They relate to the actual operation of the practice. Final budget numbers reflect adjustments that were made from the Initial Budget to meet certain goals and objectives of the practice. They also reflect realities that exist for expenses to be controlled and revenues to be realized.

- **Percent of revenue.** This column represents the final budgeted total for each expense item as a percent to the total net collections of revenue (ie, net collections).

Two totaling lines are at the bottom of the Budget Planning Worksheet. The first totaling line is the *Total for Expenses*. This simply adds each of the expense items for each particular column. The final totaling line is the *Net Income Prior to Physician Compensation*. This is the difference between the total net collections and total expenses for each column. In all instances, the Budget Planning Worksheet figures are prior to any consideration for any physician compensation, regardless of whether physicians are operating on a guaranteed income as an employee or are owners. If the physicians are owners, the figures are also prior to any consideration of any guaranteed wage or monthly draw for physician compensation.

Beginning the Budget Planning Worksheet

To begin the Budget Planning Worksheet, complete the columns that require actual information, as follows:

- Completing the budget requires both detailed analysis and planning. For each line item on the budget, look at previous financial reports for amounts that were historically spent. Be careful not to assume that just because the practice has always spent $500 per year for magazines, newspapers, and publications that it is a necessary expenditure. Instead, examine and question the expense in order to plan. What is the value of this expense? Who reads the materials? What would happen if we cut the expense to $100 per year?

- Enter all the titles of expense categories under the Items column of the Budget Planning Worksheet.

- Enter the actual dollar amount spent in each of the last three years.

- Calculate the percent of change for each item for each year and enter this percent into the Percent Change column.

- Apply the percent of change to last year's dollar amount, and enter the dollar figure in the Initial Budget column. (Remember, this is simply a calculated amount based upon prior years' actual results and trends, and is only used as a starting point from which to complete detailed analysis to formulate the Final Budget figure.)

The result of these calculations is an *unadjusted* budget figure for revenue (ie, *net collections*) and each expense for the coming year.

Completing the Final Budget

Completing the final budgeted totals requires more detailed analysis and planning. For example, review each expense line (ie, both historical results and future projections). Consider expenses and revenues in broad terms, such as patient comfort, employee job enrichment, and so on. Relate these to specific expenses in order to understand how the final budget is determined.

First, look at Fixed Expenses (ie, those not affected by patient volume). On the Budget Planning Worksheet, enter the actual dollar amount spent during the previous three years; then calculate the *Percent Change;* and finally, enter the actual amount in the *Initial Budget* column. If a contractual change is anticipated (eg, a new janitorial contract) that will affect the monthly and annual charge from previous expenses, enter that total.

For example, if salaries were $165,900 in 1999; $171,800 in 2000; and $159,700 in 2001, you have experienced a 3.6% increase from 2000 versus 1999 and 7.0% percent decrease from 2001 versus 2000. Obviously, the most recent year's decrease of 7.0% holds more weight than the previous year's 3.6% increase in deriving the Initial Budget total versus an average of the two years. Thus, use the most recent year's increase, assuming that trend will continue. With that assumption, the Initial Budget total for 2002 for salaries is $165,100, a slight increase undoubtedly for merit raises and other compensation. Post this amount in the Initial Budget column.

The result of completing the calculations for all Fixed Expenses is an unadjusted or Initial Budget total for those items.

TABLE 7-1

Budget Planning Worksheet

Items	1999	2000	% Change	2001	% Change	2002 Initial Budget	2002 Final Budget	% of Revenue
Net Collections*								
Accounting/Legal								
Contributions								
Dues/Subscriptions								
Equipment Rental								
General Insurance								
Health Insurance								
Malpractice Insurance								
Janitorial								
Medical Supplies								
Office Supplies								
Rent or Lease								
Salaries								
Taxes-Payroll								
Taxes-Other								
Telephone								
Postage								
Maintenance, Repairs								
Interest								
Depreciation								
Professional Services								
Profit Sharing								
Other								
Total Expenses								
Net Income (Before Physician Compensation, Benefits)								

* *Net Collections* represent the actual monies received and deposited into the practice. It considers the effect of discounts and contractual adjustments or write-offs from gross billings. It includes Billings or Gross Charges Less Discounts; Gross Revenue Less Write-offs; on the cash basis, Revenue Net Collections.

Forecasting Patient Volume

Before Variable Expenses can be accurately projected, it must first be determined how Patient Volume will change. Patient Volume must be considered before resuming the analysis of the Budget Planning Worksheet and Variable Expenses. To establish a basis to forecast Patient Volume, answer the following questions:

- What patient volume trends have developed throughout the past three years? Is the average percent of change in patient volume for the past two years expected to continue?

TABLE 7-2

Budget Planning Worksheet

Items	1999	2000	% Change	2001	% Change	2002 Initial Budget	2002 Final Budget	% of Revenue
Net Collections*	759,400	748,500	−1.4	736,600	−1.6	712,000	750,000	100.00%
Accounting/Legal	8,000	5,800	−27.5	5,500	−5.2	5,400	5,400	0.72
Contributions	2,500	5,000	100.0	600	−88.0	600	1,000	0.13
Dues/Subscriptions	2,000	2,500	25.0	2,000	−20.0	2,000	2,000	0.27
Equipment Rental	0	0	0.0	15,500	-	15,000	15,000	2.00
General Insurance	46,800	47,300	1.1	49,800	5.3	50,000	51,000	6.80
Health Insurance	33,600	18,100	−46.1	9,800	−45.9	10,200	10,200	1.36
Malpractice Insurance	15,900	20,400	28.3	19,700	−3.4	20,000	20,500	2.73
Janitorial	1,500	1,600	6.7	1,600	0.0	1,600	1,600	0.21
Medical Supplies	15,400	17,800	15.6	10,600	−40.4	12,000	10,000	1.33
Office Supplies	29,300	28,800	−1.7	8,500	−70.5	8,500	7,000	0.93
Rent or Lease	49,700	49,100	−1.2	44,100	−10.2	49,700	49,700	6.63
Salaries	165,900	171,800	3.6	159,700	−7.0	165,000	145,000	19.33
Taxes-Payroll	32,100	33,200	3.4	31,900	−3.9	33,000	29,000	3.87
Taxes-Other	2,200	4,700	113.6	7,500	59.6	8,000	8,000	1.07
Telephone	22,500	24,700	9.8	22,600	−8.5	23,000	23,000	3.07
Postage	5,300	7,700	45.3	7,700	0.0	8,300	8,300	1.11
Maintenance, Repairs	4,800	4,900	2.1	5,500	12.2	6,000	6,000	0.80
Interest	7,300	5,100	−30.1	4,900	−3.9	4,500	4,500	0.60
Depreciation	7,500	8,400	12.0	8,000	−4.8	8,000	8,000	1.07
Professional Services	9,400	16,700	77.7	33,800	102.4	35,000	30,000	4.00
Profit Sharing	16,700	1,000	−94.0	1,800	80.0	1,900	1,900	0.25
Other	800	1,600	100.0	15,500	868.8	10,000	5,000	0.67
Total Expenses	479,200	476,200	−0.6%	466,600	−2.0%	477,700	442,100	58.95%
Net Income (Before Physician Compensation, Benefits)	280,200	272,300	−2.8%	270,000	−0.8%	234,300	307,900	41.05%

* *Net Collections* represent the actual monies received and deposited into the practice. It considers the effect of discounts and contractual adjustments or write-offs from gross billings. It includes Billings or Gross Charges Less Discounts; Gross Revenue Less Write-offs; on the cash basis, Revenue Net Collections.

- Will there be any significant changes in managed care contracting that will result in an increase, decrease, or discontinuation of contracts, resulting in less volume?
- Will the practice add a mid-level provider (ie, Physician Assistant [PA], Nurse Practitioner [NP]) to the practice? If so, what potential effect will this have on patient volume?
- Does the practice plan to discontinue a service (eg, obstetrical care) that could decrease patient volume? Conversely, are there services that can be added to the practice that will increase patient volume?
- How many hours per day and how many days per week will the physician(s) conduct their office practice?

- What does competition dictate as far as the particular specialty of the practice? Have additional physicians in your specialty moved into the market area, presenting new competition?

- What is the marketing plan to promote the practice for the coming year? A more aggressive marketing approach should increase volume. Obviously, the cost versus the projected volume increase must be weighed.

- How far out are appointments being scheduled? If the wait seems unreasonable to the patients (for a non-emergency call), expect them to look for another physician. Here is a reason to consider either hiring a PA or NP or extending your practice hours.

For a personal application, assume the following about your practice and its competition:

- Your practice is well-established in the community and you have a high level of recognition and credibility. Managed care has increased your patient base by 300 covered lives through your first HMO contract. From your discussions with the HMO, you anticipate an addition of eight patients per month to the practice.

- Your patient volume has remained essentially constant throughout the past three years, outside of the increased managed care business, and no appreciable increase in patient volume is expected for 2002.

- A new physician in your specialty has just been recruited to the community and will set up practice less than ten miles away. From all indications, the practice could pull away some of your patients, if for no other reason than geographical proximity.

This illustration of forecasting patient volume is simple and factored on an easily determined set of circumstances. However, give careful consideration to the entire market area to determine any other factors that will affect patient volume.

Continuing with this example, based upon your research, use the historical results of a flat patient volume variance throughout the past three years, along with the increased managed care business. We will assume that the managed care contract will be a discounted fee-for-service (ie, noncapitated) contract. With capitation, the revenues from this contract may actually be easier to project than otherwise. We assume that, based on practice history, there will be no increase in patient volume. However, through managed care, we can project eight new patients per month (ie, 96 per year). Based on a projected $100 per patient average fee, the result is a revenue increase of $800 per month (ie, $9,600 per year).

Also consider that you may lose as many as ten patients per month to the new physician during the first six months. You estimate that this will level off during the last six months of the year to no more than three patients per month. Therefore, forecast your patient attrition (loss) at six patients per month or 72 per year. Thus, you estimate a loss of 72 visits and a gain of 96 visits for a *net gain of 24 patient visits for the year.*

With the flat projection for standard patient volume, your overall projected increase in patient visits in the coming year is 24. If we chart this, based on patient visits alone, the result is a small net increase in patient visits for the coming year.

This is merely one example of how such a forecast can be completed and quantified. This total is then converted into a dollar amount to derive total patient volume for the year. This must then be converted, based upon contractual obligations and write-offs in order to derive a *net collected cash total,* upon which the Budget Planning Worksheet is based.

In summary, many factors affect the number of patients seen. The practice cannot assume that patient volume will increase every year. Remember that in our example, we actually assumed no increase before considering other new factors (ie, the new managed care contract and the new practice). The more aware the practice is of what is going on in its market area and the industry in general, the more accurately it can forecast changes.

The real benefit of a well-planned practice budget comes from careful consideration of changes and the ability to accurately reflect or forecast these upon the practice operations.

Forecasting Variable Expenses

By forecasting Patient Volume, we can more accurately forecast the expenses that will change with that volume. The first step in forecasting *Variable Expenses* is to calculate the current cost per patient. To accomplish this, refer to Patient Cost Analysis examples in Table 7-3 and Table 7-4. Table 7-4 gives the appropriate entries and calculations to derive a revenue per patient total.

T A B L E 7-3

Patient (Variable) Cost Analysis

1. Total number of patients seen for prior 12 months	_____
2. Total of all nonphysician/provider expenses for prior 12 months	_____
3. Subtract from line 2 all **Fixed Expenses** (eg, rent, salaries, benefits, insurance, utilities)	_____
4. Total **Patient** expenses (ie, variable expenses) for prior 12 months	_____
5. Total receipts for prior 12 months	_____
6. Divide line 5 by line 1 to get collections per patient	_____
7. Divide line 4 by line 1 to variable expenses per patient	_____
8. Subtract line 7 from line 6 to get variable margin per patient	_____

T A B L E 7-4

Patient Cost Analysis

1. Total number of patients seen for prior 12 months	15,600
2. Total of all nonphysician/provider expenses for prior 12 months	$600,000.00
3. Subtract from line 2 all **Fixed Expenses** (eg, rent, salaries, benefits, insurance, utilities)	$480,000.00
4. Total **Patient** expenses (ie, variable expenses) for prior 12 months	$120,000.00
5. Total receipts for prior 12 months	$1,000,000.00
6. Divide line 5 by line 1 to get collections per patient	$64.10
7. Divide line 4 by line 1 to get variable expenses per patient	$7.69
8. Subtract line 7 from line 6 to get variable margin per patient	$56.41

The following is a review of each line item of this example:

- **Line Item 1: Total Number of Patients Seen for Prior 12 Months**

  This should be the actual office visits recorded by the physician(s). Unless you are performing these projections at the end of your current fiscal period, it would be more accurate to use the last 12 months' data.

- **Line Item 2: Total of All Expenses for the Prior 12 Months**

  This is an entry directly off your financial statements. It should not include compensation or benefit to the physician(s) or any other providers.

- **Line Item 3: Fixed Expenses**

  Fixed expenses, such as rent, salaries, insurance, and utilities, should be subtracted from Line 2 to derive this entry.

- **Line Item 4: Total Patient Expense (ie, Variable Expenses)**

  This includes all other expenses that in theory change with volume of encounters.

- **Line Item 5: Actual Cash Receipts for the Prior 12 Months**

- **Line Item 6: Gross Collections Per Patient**

  This is calculated by dividing Line Number 5 by Line Number 1. In our example, the $64.10 total revenue per patient is calculated.

- **Line Item 7: Variable Cost Per Patient**

  This is calculated by dividing Line Number 4, Total Patient Expenses, by Line Number 1, Total Number of Patients Seen for Prior 12 Months.

- **Line Item 8: Variable Margin Per Patient**

  This is the subtraction of Line Number 7 from Line Number 6.

Forecasting Revenue

As noted, determining patient volume is the first step in forecasting revenue. Consider both internal and external anticipated changes within the practice to develop a logical projection of patient visits for the coming year.

Another component in forecasting revenue is to determine if and how much of an increase in the fee schedule the practice plans to make. At a minimum, a practice should adjust its fees at the beginning of each year. This can be accomplished by two simple methods:

- Apply a percent of increase to every fee, based upon inflation, an inflation index, a cost of living change, or specific factors in the individual practice that ultimately dictate an adjustment. Also, reflect any adjustments to Medicare's fee schedule in this analysis.

- Review each fee and increase those that have increased in cost to deliver.

Knowing costs is a significant component of successfully negotiating and securing a managed care contract. A fee schedule can be based upon such contracting. Although fee schedules may vary by payer type (eg, indemnity insurance, Medicare, HMO, PPO managed care), it is best to have a consistent fee schedule that changes to accommodate different types of payers. However, practice management software allows the user to input different fee schedules for each managed care plan. The software enters the proper fee initially, eliminating the need for adjustments.

Competition is another factor to consider when making a change in the fee schedule. It is helpful to know what your competition is charging for comparable services. Remember, it is likely acceptable to *shop* competitive prices (ie, informally, on a limited basis), but it is probably illegal for practices to agree to uniform their pricing schedule.

Though it may be difficult to anticipate the effect of a fee schedule change in the budget planning process, a safe approach is to apply a 2% to 3% cost of living adjustment for inflation. Budgeting is primarily for internal use and requires a realistic approach. If a fee schedule is certain to increase by more than a simple cost of living adjustment, reflect that in the budget. However, if it is not a certainty, particularly when completing the Budget Planning Worksheet, then a simple increase may be justified. On the other hand, if managed care contracting will result in lowering the fee schedule, then this should be realistically reflected in the projections as well.

Another step in forecasting revenue is to determine if the practice plans to offer new services to generate additional revenue. For example, the practice might purchase a flexible sigmoidoscope to perform sigmoidoscopy screening in the office. Some historical information will be needed to accurately project revenues that the new service might generate. If it is not available, then realistic projections must be used. For example, historical information might tell you that the practice performed 100 sigmoidoscopies last year and referred another 50 patients to the outpatient gastroenterology center at the hospital.

If you could project that the practice will do 100 sigmoidoscopies next year, based on the 300 complete physical examinations conducted last year, then you can assume that at least one in three of those would need a sigmoidoscopy as a screening procedure. The average reimbursement for *CPT Code 45330 Sigmoidoscopy Flexible Fiber Optic Diagnostic* is approximately $150. With the projection of doing 100 sigmoidoscopies at $150, the practice will realize an estimated *$15,000* in additional revenue.

Your projections determine that revenues will increase at a 3% inflation rate over the prior year due to an across-the-board fee schedule increase. Thus, 3% of the estimated $1,000,000 base revenue results in $30,000 additional revenue for the new year.

Add to this figure the revenue you would gain from the previously projected increase in patient volume (eg, assume the 24 new patients × $64.10 or $1,538.40 in additional revenue). (Note: The $64.10 revenue per patient is a result of our previous calculation of gross revenue per patient completed in Table 7-4.)

Altogether the three increases will provide $46,538.40 in added revenues to be budgeted in the next year:

Added Services $15,000.00
Fee Increases 30,000.00
New Patients 1,538.40
Total **$46,538.40**

This amount is reflected in the Budget Planning Worksheet, *Initial Budget* column.

Now that forecasting patient volume has been reviewed, Variable Expenses (ie, those that change with patient volume and can be projected in a step-by-step process) can be considered.

Step One is to determine the level of cost increase expected for each of the Variable Expenses. For example, ask the question, "What was the average percent of increase for medical supplies throughout the last three years?" Refer to your Budget Planning Worksheet (Tables 7-1 and 7-2) for this entry. A sensible follow-up question would be, "Is it reasonable to expect that the cost of supplies for the coming year will increase as much as they have throughout the past three years?" If the answer to this question is yes, then it is appropriate to include the average percentage increase over last year's figure to develop next year's Initial Budget total.

In the example, a slight increase in Patient Volume was forecast. This requires consideration of an obvious increase in the cost of seeing patients. The simplest method is to take the cost per patient, calculated for each patient last year on the Patient Cost Analysis Worksheet (see Table 7-4), and multiply this dollar amount by the projected net gain of patients. For example, earlier we projected a net gain of 24 patients for the new year. In Table 7-4, we calculated the prior year's average cost per patient as $7.69. Multiply the 24 patients by $7.69 to determine a total cost of $184.56 to see these additional patients.

Next, determine the number of Variable Expenses categories. If there are five, divide the total reached in the above calculation by five and enter an equal amount of the increase to each of these five expense categories. For example, assume that the only Variable Expenses are office supplies, medical supplies, laboratory expenses, X-ray expenses, and transcription fees. Because of their nature, they all change with patient volume. In this exercise, $184.56 divided by 5 equals $36.91—the total to be added to each column. Now, add $36.91 to each of the five expense categories. The amounts vary according to the number of Variable Expenses categories.

To complete the Budget Planning Worksheet Initial Budget column, convert to dollars the percent of increase you have determined for each Variable Expense. For example, medical supply costs have increased an average of 2% throughout the last three years. Assume that you will experience the same level of increase next year. Medical supply costs last year were $10,600, so increase this figure by 2%, or to $10,812. Add to this the $36.91, the determined cost for medical supplies, to see the addition of the 24 new patients. The total budgeted amount for medical supplies will then be $10,848.91.

Final Budget Column Entries

With all the calculations and inputs complete for the Initial Budget column, the Final Budget figure is now becoming more clear. Before proceeding, take time to consider all other factors within the practice that will influence the Final Budget total. These factors might include a realistic overview of what is going on within the practice or the knowledge of an external or internal factor that will significantly change the initial budgeted total to the final entry. The key decision-makers should review each line entry to formulate the Final Budget. Remember, regardless of how thoroughly analyzed a budget might be, it requires a total buy-in by the physician(s) and/or other owners of the practice to be taken seriously and to be used as the management tool for which it is intended.

The Final Step

Now that you have arrived at a realistic budget figure for each projected expense and the operating revenues, the final step is to calculate the percent of each expense to total revenue projected. It is important to interpret all budgeted data, especially expense entries, on a line-by-line basis. Also, it is essential to convert expenses as a percent of total net collections. Many of the industry-published guidelines are only reflected as a percent of collections. For example, a practice that operates at 50% or less expense factor (ie, 50% of net collections for total expenses, excluding physician compensation) is generally viewed as having a fairly efficient structure. Conversely, a budget that results in an expense total in excess of 50% requires further research to ascertain if this is acceptable. Historically, if a practice has operated on an expense factor of 55% to 60% of net collections, the physician(s) and/or other owners of the practice may find this acceptable. If the owners do not object, the final budget may reflect a higher than (industry) standard expense total.

Expense-to-earnings percentages vary with geographical locations, the specialty, and the type of practice, such as solo versus group. The benchmark figures for your specialty are available from several sources (eg, the American Medical Group Association, Medical Group Management Association, local consulting firms). In addition, *Medical Economics* magazine publishes these expense averages each year in its November issue.

The final step of calculating the percentages of each expense item to total net collections is a process that brings the budgeted figures into perspective.

The Reality Check

The outcome of completing the Budget Planning Worksheet is a true internal assessment of the practice. In other words, it becomes the reality check.

After the budget is set and complete with final entries, the practice administrator and physician(s) should look at the totals taken as a whole. Previously, it was noted that the percentages of expense items to net collections is an ongoing process throughout the formulation of the budget and should not necessarily be delayed until the budget is complete. However, when all of the numbers are entered and the calculations made with the totals set for the budget, it is logical and sensible to take a broad view at the outcome in relation to the reality of running the practice.

The Reality Check should ask the following questions for each entry:

- Is this entry realistic?
- Can we afford the increases or decreases?
- Will the increases maintain the practice at a competitive level and result in efficient operation comparable to prior years?
- What does management (ie, the physician[s]) really want?

Another part of the Reality Check is to analyze if the expenses are reasonable in light of where the practice is going and what has traditionally been acceptable performance. Physicians are sometimes more interested in maintaining a certain level of quality or prestige in their practice than being concerned about the costs to maintain their standards. For example, certain practice commodities are not necessary, such as providing a coffee service, bottled water, and other niceties. Logically, a practice under pressure to cut expenses would cut nonessentials first. Before cutting or eliminating these expenses, however, the physician(s) must be consulted and agree. It is futile to cut the budget for items that realistically will not be enacted.

Part of the Reality Check is converting the numbers to real-time running the day-to-day practice. A budget is not useful or beneficial unless it reflects actual day-to-day occurrences and expenses. It is essential to link the numbers on a Budget with the realities of the practice's operations. Reluctance to make the connection from paper to reality renders the entire budgeting process useless.

Incorporating the Budget into the Monthly Income Statement

When you are satisfied that your budget figures are as accurate and realistic as possible, ask your accounting professional or firm to add these figures to your Monthly Income Statement. Then, each month, you will have a comparison of the actual figures to the budgeted amounts. (Table 7-5 is a sample Income Statement with columns for budget and variance.)

With monthly monitoring of the actual operating results with the budgeted figures as an essential process, this becomes a *working budget*, not one that is completed and placed on a shelf with no further consideration.

If monthly actual results are noticed that are considerably higher or lower than the budgeted figures, do not overreact. Simply research the variances to determine why they occurred. Closely monitor the results for a couple of months to determine real trends. Frequently unexpected results will level out through the course of the year. Remember that a budget that is properly set up is a useful management tool that gives early exposure to either negative or positive trends. Do not wait too long to bring variances to the attention of the physician(s), and be prepared to satisfactorily

TABLE 7-5

Income Statement

	Current Month			Year-to-Date		
	Budget	**Actual**	**% Variance**	**Budget**	**Actual**	**% Variance**
Income						
Charges						
Other Adjustments						
Other Receipts						
Total Income						
Expenses						
Salaries (office)						
Answering Service and Pager						
Automobile						
Consultant Fees						
Conventions and Meetings						
Contributions						
Depreciation						
Dues/Subscriptions						
Employee Benefits						
Gifts/Flowers						
Insurance (business)						
Insurance (malpractice)						
Laundry (uniforms)						
Legal and Accounting						
Medical Pamphlets and Books						
Miscellaneous						
Office Supplies and Expense						
Postage						
Profit Sharing						
Rent						
Repairs and Maintenance						
Supplies (medical)						
Taxes and Licenses						
Telephone						
Transcription Fees						
X-ray Expense						
Total Expenses						
Operating Income <Loss>						

present the reasons for the variances. Complete a summary to supplement the monthly financial statements given to the physician(s) that explain the significant variances. The key is to always research monthly overages or shortages to see why an unexpected result has occurred.

When the budgeted totals are prepared with care and forethought (ie, realistic and accurate), their comparison to actual results bears more analytical weight than comparisons with actual prior year's totals. After the process is completed and incorporated into the financial statement process, it forms the basis of future decision-making.

Physicians are facing dramatic health care reform that will continue into the future. It is now necessary to operate more cost effectively. The increasing pressure to discount fees for large blocks of patients is expected to continue. Increasing the physicians' income, as well as limiting expenses, will be more important than ever to the operation and management of a medical practice.

Financial management in the medical practice requires a firm commitment to planning and budgeting to sustain the practice operation. Medical practices are complex business operations that face increasing challenges to making a profit. Planning, which is formalized in a budget, helps produce a successful and profitable practice.

Zero-Based Budgeting

As a business develops and matures, the budgeting process becomes more predictable. An existing practice that has been operating for a number of years will merely complete its budget based mainly upon the prior year's performance. This is acceptable to a point, yet it is also appropriate to reconsider this process at least every two to three years. Within that context, we introduce the concept of zero-based budgeting.

Zero-based budgeting is a time-consuming project that requires commitment from the entire organization.

Zero-based budgeting is the process that examines all budget items from zero. It requires that every level of expenditure greater than zero be supported. It focuses on the actual delivery of services or procedures. All activities are questioned and evaluated as follows:

- Should the activity be performed?
- What is the cost required to perform the activity?
- Are we doing too much?
- What are alternative approaches for achieving the objectives?

Thus, the zero-based budgeting process forces managers to understand cost allocation and explore alternative methods for accomplishing the required objectives. It does not assume that history is always right. Just because a certain amount of expense was incurred in the past (eg, office supplies, rent, salaries), does not always justify those expenditures in the future. The zero-based budgeting process takes a fresh look at all expenses. It requires renewed accountability. It entails all the managers as well as the owners of the business to refocus on expenses to determine their justification for the future. Zero-based budgeting is much like the start of a new business, where all expenses are examined with discretion and analysis.

The most common steps to implement a zero-based budget are:

- List every service and procedure that is performed in the year under consideration
- Rank the services and procedures in order of priority
- Identify every item of cost that pertains to each service or procedure
- Conduct a formal cost assessment of each element of expense

Focus on renewed accountability. Do not assume an expense is justified just because "it had always been done that way."

The zero-based budget cost assessment process should answer the following questions:

- How much should it cost?
- Can we buy the required resources for less than what we are currently paying?
- How can we do that?

The end result of the zero-based budget may be surprising. In some respects, in comparison to the traditional budgeting process, line items may be quite comparable. In other ways, line items may be significantly different, usually much lower. The end result is a much more effective way to regulate costs, which is a positive aspect to efficient management. Moreover, it compels all members of the organization to rethink their justification for incurring an expense and/or performing a certain service.

The zero-based budget does have some drawbacks. It is more time-consuming than a traditional budget and it may be more useful for organizations that are project or procedure oriented. Thus, the traditional medical practice whose processes, services, and products vary little from year to year may not need frequent zero-based budgeting and may not greatly benefit. It also requires a total commitment from the physicians in leadership positions within the practice.

A zero-based budget is an excellent management tool that should be introduced after the practice or other health care entity has been operating for at least two to three years, and should be repeated every two to three years (or more often if services change significantly).

PRO FORMA STATEMENTS

A major part of the budgeting process is the development of pro forma statements (ie, usually pro forma, cash flow, and income statements). Pro formas are a focused initiative within the budgeting process. Pro forma projections are for a specific initiative, similar to and as a part of the business plan. For example, a medical practice is entertaining the idea of adding a satellite location, which includes the consideration of adding a new physician/provider for that site. Although this is a budgeting function, making the decision requires a detailed analysis of the financial operating performance, as in the completion of a pro forma cash flow and income statement.

As another example, if an organization considers adding an ancillary service, such as the delivery of specific professional services, tests, or procedures, the organization's business plan would entail a pro forma projection.

The pro forma will consider all types of costs, both initial and ongoing, and it will consider the potential for and amount of revenue that can be generated from the specific venture. Pro formas should consider the following areas:

- Start-up costs
- Inventory
- Furniture and equipment
- Software and hardware (ie, computer information system)
- Education
- Marketing
- Compliance issues
- Site preparation
- Ongoing expenses
- Variable expenses
- Fixed expenses
- Revenue
- Gross charges
- Net charges
- Net collections
- RVUs

Like the budget, the pro forma is a projection of the ongoing income, expenses, and cash flow on a month-to-month basis; however, the pro forma may be much more detailed. The pro forma provides critical answers, as follows:

- What is the likely return on investment?
- Is this worth the risk?
- What is the justification for the expansion?
- What is the payback period to return the initial investment to the owners?

The pro forma will also help organize and determine the need for start-up capital and is often a lender-required and scrutinized part of the business plan. Lenders want to see the pro forma financials to make sure that the owners have considered all possible costs and revenues of the venture. In addition, lenders want to see these questions answered themselves, as well as for the business owner.

Thus, the pro forma is a wonderful tool to be used both internally and externally for the new business owner or the current owners as they consider a specific initiative.

Preparation of the Pro Forma

Preferably, an independent party should complete the pro forma, unless the practice has sufficient expertise within its organization to complete this review. An independent party introduces an element of objectivity that results in more realistic projections. The more realistic the projections, the more beneficial they will be to the user (both externally and internally).

Typically, the process should start with an outline of projected revenues and expenses, itemized as in the budgeting process. A major difference is that there is little, if any, history to go by in making such projections. Industry benchmarks and other data from comparable initiatives are useful. An experienced consultant will have access to industry benchmarks that are appropriate for pro forma projections. The pro forma will include well-documented assumptions as to revenue and expenses.

As far as revenue is concerned, typical assumptions should include the number of procedures, the number of providers doing the procedures, the expected reimbursement per procedure or encounter, the expected net reimbursement after discounting, and other key areas typical to the projection of revenue.

Likewise, expenses should be allocated based upon both fixed and variable costs. Fixed costs will not change regardless of the projected volume. Variable expenses will change as volume changes, and may be stated as a percentage of each dollar of revenue.

Normally, the pro forma's projection is broken down on a month-to-month basis, preferably, for the first two to three years of performance.

The actual pro forma will look like a typical financial statement or cash flow statement. The statement of cash flow should be stated on a true cash basis (ie, without noncash items, such as depreciation) and should show the flow of cash. The cash flow to be shown will be both from the beginning of the first month through the end of the last month in consideration (eg, for two years, this would be 24 months). The income statement is more traditional in that it illustrates each month's performance somewhat independent of all others. The pro forma income statement and cash flow should also show a line item of physician or provider compensation, if applicable, as well as the cost of borrowing the initial start-up or capital required.

An appropriate application for a pro forma financial statement is the start-up of a new medical practice. Table 7-6 illustrates examples of pro forma financial statements for a practice start-up. The examples include the end result of both the cash flow projection throughout two years and an income statement.

The pro forma provides needed information about a new enterprise or initiative. For example, it will indicate when cumulative cash flow will become positive, showing when all debt will be repaid. It indicates when profitability will be attained and the amount that can be expected. It will provide the answers to the projected return on investment. Lastly, it will provide to owners and prospective investors/lenders the maximum amounts of money that will be needed, which will include requirements for both line of credit and start-up capital.

TABLE 7-6

Statement of Cash Flow: Year One

	Month 1	Month 2	Month 3	Month 4	Month 5	Month 6	Month 7	Month 8	Month 9	Month 10	Month 11	Month 12	Totals
Beginning Cash Balance	$0	($63,714)	($76,847)	($80,401)	($79,010)	($77,364)	($75,460)	($73,295)	($70,866)	($68,169)	($65,203)	($61,964)	$0
Receipts													
Professional Fees Collected	$20,666	$36,268	$46,782	$52,183	$52,444	$52,706	$52,969	$53,234	$53,500	$53,768	$54,037	$54,307	$582,864
Other Income	$0	$0	$0	$0	$0	$0	$0	$0	$0	$0	$0	$0	$0
Total Receipts (Inflow)	$20,666	$36,268	$46,782	$52,183	$52,444	$52,706	$52,969	$53,234	$53,500	$53,768	$54,037	$54,307	$582,864
Total Cash Inflows													
Expenses													
Staff Salaries	$13,363	$13,363	$13,363	$13,363	$13,363	$13,363	$13,363	$13,363	$13,363	$13,363	$13,363	$13,363	$160,357
Payroll Taxes	$1,203	$1,203	$1,203	$1,203	$1,203	$1,203	$1,203	$1,203	$1,203	$1,203	$1,203	$1,203	$14,432
Insurances													
Group Health	$2,520	$2,520	$2,520	$2,520	$2,520	$2,520	$2,520	$2,520	$2,520	$2,520	$2,520	$2,520	$30,240
Group Disability	$0	$0	$0	$0	$0	$0	$0	$0	$0	$0	$0	$0	$0
Group Life	$67	$67	$67	$67	$67	$67	$67	$67	$67	$67	$67	$67	$800
Group Dental	$236	$236	$236	$236	$236	$236	$236	$236	$236	$236	$236	$236	$2,832
Pension Administration	$0	$0	$0	$0	$0	$0	$0	$0	$0	$0	$0	$0	$0
Pension Plan	$0	$0	$0	$0	$0	$0	$0	$0	$0	$0	$0	$0	$0
Profit Sharing	$0	$0	$0	$0	$0	$0	$0	$0	$0	$0	$0	$0	$0
Patient Education Materials	$0	$0	$0	$0	$0	$0	$0	$0	$0	$0	$0	$0	$0
Billing and Collections	$1,653	$2,901	$3,743	$4,175	$4,195	$4,216	$4,238	$4,259	$4,280	$4,301	$4,323	$4,345	$46,629
Bank Charges	$208	$208	$208	$208	$208	$208	$208	$208	$208	$208	$208	$208	$2,500
Continuing Education (staff)	$50	$50	$50	$50	$50	$50	$50	$50	$50	$50	$50	$50	$600
Continuing Education (physician)	$167	$167	$167	$167	$167	$167	$167	$167	$167	$167	$167	$167	$2,000

	Month 1	Month 2	Month 3	Month 4	Month 5	Month 6	Month 7	Month 8	Month 9	Month 10	Month 11	Month 12	Totals
Computer Depreciation	$0	$0	$0	$0	$0	$0	$0	$0	$0	$0	$0	$0	$0
Asset Depreciation	$0	$0	$0	$0	$0	$0	$0	$0	$0	$0	$0	$0	$0
Drugs/ Immunizations	$1,583	$1,583	$1,583	$1,583	$1,583	$1,583	$1,583	$1,583	$1,583	$1,583	$1,583	$1,583	$19,000
Gifts	$17	$17	$17	$17	$17	$17	$17	$17	$17	$17	$17	$17	$200
Insurance (physician) Malpractice	$210	$210	$210	$210	$210	$210	$210	$210	$210	$210	$210	$210	$2,514
Insurance (other) Malpractice	$0	$0	$0	$0	$0	$0	$0	$0	$0	$0	$0	$0	$0
Laboratory Fees	$67	$67	$67	$67	$67	$67	$67	$67	$67	$67	$67	$67	$800
Interest Expense (loan)	$0	$0	$0	$0	$0	$0	$0	$0	$0	$0	$0	$0	$0
Licenses and Dues	$250	$250	$250	$250	$250	$250	$250	$250	$250	$250	$250	$250	$3,000
Maintenance and Repair (general)	$475	$475	$475	$475	$475	$475	$475	$475	$475	$475	$475	$475	$5,700
Meals	$29	$29	$29	$29	$29	$29	$29	$29	$29	$29	$29	$29	$350
Meetings/ Conferences	$29	$29	$29	$29	$29	$29	$29	$29	$29	$29	$29	$29	$350
Medical Supplies	$808	$808	$808	$808	$808	$808	$808	$808	$808	$808	$808	$808	$9,700
Office Maintenance	$183	$183	$183	$183	$183	$183	$183	$183	$183	$183	$183	$183	$2,200
Office Supplies	$833	$833	$833	$833	$833	$833	$833	$833	$833	$833	$833	$833	$10,000
Postage	$208	$208	$208	$208	$208	$208	$208	$208	$208	$208	$208	$208	$2,500
Professional Services	$750	$750	$750	$750	$750	$750	$750	$750	$750	$750	$750	$750	$9,000
Promotion/ Advertising	$333	$333	$333	$333	$333	$333	$333	$333	$333	$333	$333	$333	$4,000

continued

TABLE 7-6 continued

Statement of Cash Flow: Year One

	Month 1	Month 2	Month 3	Month 4	Month 5	Month 6	Month 7	Month 8	Month 9	Month 10	Month 11	Month 12	Totals
Rental/Leased Equipment	$0	$0	$0	$0	$0	$0	$0	$0	$0	$0	$0	$0	$0
Rent (facility)	$2,709	$2,709	$2,709	$2,709	$2,709	$2,709	$2,709	$2,709	$2,709	$2,709	$2,709	$2,709	$32,505
Subscriptions/Books	$58	$58	$58	$58	$58	$58	$58	$58	$58	$58	$58	$58	$700
Taxes (start-up)	$0	$0	$0	$0	$0	$0	$0	$0	$0	$0	$0	$0	$0
Telephone	$417	$417	$417	$417	$417	$417	$417	$417	$417	$417	$417	$417	$5,000
Travel	$0	$0	$0	$0	$0	$0	$0	$0	$0	$0	$0	$0	$0
Utilities	$1,082	$1,082	$1,082	$1,082	$1,082	$1,082	$1,082	$1,082	$1,082	$1,082	$1,082	$1,082	$12,980
Start-up Equipment Cost	$36,705	$0	$0	$0	$0	$0	$0	$0	$0	$0	$0	$0	$36,705
Total Cash Outflow	$66,213	$30,756	$31,598	$32,030	$32,051	$32,071	$32,093	$32,114	$32,135	$32,156	$32,178	$32,200	$417,594
Net Cash Flow Before Draw	($45,547)	$5,512	$15,185	$20,153	$20,393	$20,634	$20,877	$21,120	$21,365	$21,611	$21,859	$22,107	$165,270
Physician Draw	$16,667	$16,667	$16,667	$16,667	$16,667	$16,667	$16,667	$16,667	$16,667	$16,667	$16,667	$16,667	$200,000
Physician Payroll Taxes	$1,500	$1,500	$1,500	$1,500	$1,500	$1,500	$1,500	$1,500	$1,500	$1,500	$1,500	$1,500	$18,000
Net Cash Flow	($63,714)	($12,655)	($2,982)	$1,986	$2,226	$2,468	$2,710	$2,954	$3,199	$3,445	$3,692	$3,941	($52,730)
Ending Cash Balance Before Interest Expense	($63,714)	($76,369)	($79,829)	($78,415)	($76,784)	($74,896)	($72,750)	($70,341)	($67,667)	($64,725)	($61,511)	($58,023)	($52,730)
Interest Expense	$0	($478)	($573)	($595)	($580)	($564)	($545)	($525)	($503)	($479)	($453)	($425)	($5,718)
Ending Cash Balance	($63,714)	($76,847)	($80,401)	($79,010)	($77,364)	($75,460)	($73,295)	($70,866)	($68,169)	($65,203)	($61,964)	($58,448)	($58,448)

Statement of Cash Flow: Year Two

	Month 13	Month 14	Month 15	Month 16	Month 17	Month 18	Month 19	Month 20	Month 21	Month 22	Month 23	Month 24	Totals
Beginning Cash Balance	($58,448)	($55,898)	($53,074)	($49,974)	($46,594)	($42,932)	($38,984)	($34,747)	($30,218)	($25,393)	($20,269)	($14,844)	($58,448)
Receipts													
Professional Fees Collected	$54,578	$54,851	$55,126	$55,401	$55,678	$55,957	$56,236	$56,518	$56,800	$57,084	$57,370	$57,656	$673,256
Other Income	$0	$0	$0	$0	$0	$0	$0	$0	$0	$0	$0	$0	$0
Total Receipts (Inflow)	$54,578	$54,851	$55,126	$55,401	$55,678	$55,957	$56,236	$56,518	$56,800	$57,084	$57,370	$57,656	$673,256
Total Cash Inflows													
Expenses													
Staff Salaries	$12,793	$12,793	$12,793	$12,793	$12,793	$12,793	$12,793	$12,793	$12,793	$12,793	$12,793	$12,793	$153,510
Payroll Taxes	$1,151	$1,151	$1,151	$1,151	$1,151	$1,151	$1,151	$1,151	$1,151	$1,151	$1,151	$1,151	$13,816
Insurances													
Group Health	$2,800	$2,800	$2,800	$2,800	$2,800	$2,800	$2,800	$2,800	$2,800	$2,800	$2,800	$2,800	$33,600
Group Disability	$0	$0	$0	$0	$0	$0	$0	$0	$0	$0	$0	$0	$0
Group Life	$70	$70	$70	$70	$70	$70	$70	$70	$70	$70	$70	$70	$840
Group Dental	$255	$255	$255	$255	$255	$255	$255	$255	$255	$255	$255	$255	$3,060
Pension Administration	$0	$0	$0	$0	$0	$0	$0	$0	$0	$0	$0	$0	$0
Pension Plan	$0	$0	$0	$0	$0	$0	$0	$0	$0	$0	$0	$0	$0
Profit Sharing	$0	$0	$0	$0	$0	$0	$0	$0	$0	$0	$0	$0	$0
Patient Education Materials	$0	$0	$0	$0	$0	$0	$0	$0	$0	$0	$0	$0	$0
Billing and Collections	$4,366	$4,388	$4,410	$4,432	$4,454	$4,477	$4,499	$4,521	$4,544	$4,567	$4,590	$4,613	$53,860
Bank Charges	$250	$250	$250	$250	$250	$250	$250	$250	$250	$250	$250	$250	$3,000
Continuing Education (staff)	$53	$53	$53	$53	$53	$53	$53	$53	$53	$53	$53	$53	$630

continued

TABLE 7-6 *continued*
Statement of Cash Flow: Year Two

	Month 13	Month 14	Month 15	Month 16	Month 17	Month 18	Month 19	Month 20	Month 21	Month 22	Month 23	Month 24	Totals
Continuing Education (physician)	$167	$167	$167	$167	$167	$167	$167	$167	$167	$167	$167	$167	$2,000
Computer Depreciation	$0	$0	$0	$0	$0	$0	$0	$0	$0	$0	$0	$0	$0
Asset Depreciation	$0	$0	$0	$0	$0	$0	$0	$0	$0	$0	$0	$0	$0
Drugs/ Immunizations	$1,663	$1,663	$1,663	$1,663	$1,663	$1,663	$1,663	$1,663	$1,663	$1,663	$1,663	$1,663	$19,950
Gifts	$18	$18	$18	$18	$18	$18	$18	$18	$18	$18	$18	$18	$210
Insurance (physician) Malpractice	$220	$220	$220	$220	$220	$220	$220	$220	$220	$220	$220	$220	$2,640
Insurance (other) Malpractice	$0	$0	$0	$0	$0	$0	$0	$0	$0	$0	$0	$0	$0
Laboratory Fees	$70	$70	$70	$70	$70	$70	$70	$70	$70	$70	$70	$70	$840
Interest Expense: Loan	$0	$0	$0	$0	$0	$0	$0	$0	$0	$0	$0	$0	$0
Licenses and Dues	$263	$263	$263	$263	$263	$263	$263	$263	$263	$263	$263	$263	$3,150
Maintenance and Repair (general)	$499	$499	$499	$499	$499	$499	$499	$499	$499	$499	$499	$499	$5,985
Meals	$31	$31	$31	$31	$31	$31	$31	$31	$31	$31	$31	$31	$368
Meetings/ Conferences	$29	$29	$29	$29	$29	$29	$29	$29	$29	$29	$29	$29	$350
Medical Supplies	$849	$849	$849	$849	$849	$849	$849	$849	$849	$849	$849	$849	$10,185
Office Maintenance	$193	$193	$193	$193	$193	$193	$193	$193	$193	$193	$193	$193	$2,310
Office Supplies	$875	$875	$875	$875	$875	$875	$875	$875	$875	$875	$875	$875	$10,500
Postage	$219	$219	$219	$219	$219	$219	$219	$219	$219	$219	$219	$219	$2,625
Professional Services	$788	$788	$788	$788	$788	$788	$788	$788	$788	$788	$788	$788	$9,450

	Month 13	Month 14	Month 15	Month 16	Month 17	Month 18	Month 19	Month 20	Month 21	Month 22	Month 23	Month 24	Totals
Promotion/ Advertising	$350	$350	$350	$350	$350	$350	$350	$350	$350	$350	$350	$350	$4,200
Rental/Leased Equipment													
Rent (facility)	$2,955	$2,955	$2,955	$2,955	$2,955	$2,955	$2,955	$2,955	$2,955	$2,955	$2,955	$2,955	$35,460
Subscriptions/ Books	$61	$61	$61	$61	$61	$61	$61	$61	$61	$61	$61	$61	$735
Taxes (start-up)	$0	$0	$0	$0	$0	$0	$0	$0	$0	$0	$0	$0	$0
Telephone	$438	$438	$438	$438	$438	$438	$438	$438	$438	$438	$438	$438	$5,250
Travel	$0	$0	$0	$0	$0	$0	$0	$0	$0	$0	$0	$0	$0
Utilities	$1,136	$1,136	$1,136	$1,136	$1,136	$1,136	$1,136	$1,136	$1,136	$1,136	$1,136	$1,136	$13,629
Start-up Equipment Cost	$0	$0	$0	$0	$0	$0	$0	$0	$0	$0	$0	$0	$0
Total Cash Outflow	$32,557	$32,579	$32,601	$32,623	$32,645	$32,668	$32,690	$32,712	$32,735	$32,758	$32,781	$32,804	$392,153
Net Cash Flow Before Draw	$22,021	$22,272	$22,525	$22,778	$23,033	$23,289	$23,546	$23,805	$24,065	$24,326	$24,589	$24,853	$281,103
Physician Draw	$17,500	$17,500	$17,500	$17,500	$17,500	$17,500	$17,500	$17,500	$17,500	$17,500	$17,500	$17,500	$210,000
Physician Payroll Taxes	$1,575	$1,575	$1,575	$1,575	$1,575	$1,575	$1,575	$1,575	$1,575	$1,575	$1,575	$1,575	$18,900
Net Cash Flow	$2,946	$3,197	$3,450	$3,703	$3,958	$4,214	$4,471	$4,730	$4,990	$5,251	$5,514	$5,778	$52,203
Ending Cash Balance Before Interest Expense	($55,502)	($52,700)	($49,624)	($46,270)	($42,636)	($38,718)	($34,512)	($30,017)	($25,227)	($20,141)	($14,755)	($9,066)	($6,245)
Interest Expense	($395)	($373)	($349)	($324)	($296)	($266)	($234)	($201)	($165)	($128)	($89)	($47)	($2,868)
Ending Cash Balance	($55,898)	($53,074)	($49,974)	($46,594)	($42,932)	($38,984)	($34,747)	($30,218)	($25,393)	($20,269)	($14,844)	($9,113)	($9,113)

continued

TABLE 7-6 *continued*

Income Statement: Year One

	Month 1	Month 2	Month 3	Month 4	Month 5	Month 6	Month 7	Month 8	Month 9	Month 10	Month 11	Month 12	Totals
Income													
Professional Fees Collected	$20,666	$36,268	$46,782	$52,183	$52,444	$52,706	$52,969	$53,234	$53,500	$53,768	$54,037	$54,307	$582,864
Other Income	$0	$0	$0	$0	$0	$0	$0	$0	$0	$0	$0	$0	$0
Total Income	$20,666	$36,268	$46,782	$52,183	$52,444	$52,706	$52,969	$53,234	$53,500	$53,768	$54,037	$54,307	$582,864
Expenses													
Staff Salaries	$13,363	$13,363	$13,363	$13,363	$13,363	$13,363	$13,363	$13,363	$13,363	$13,363	$13,363	$13,363	$160,357
Payroll Taxes	$1,203	$1,203	$1,203	$1,203	$1,203	$1,203	$1,203	$1,203	$1,203	$1,203	$1,203	$1,203	$14,432
Insurances													
Group Health	$2,520	$2,520	$2,520	$2,520	$2,520	$2,520	$2,520	$2,520	$2,520	$2,520	$2,520	$2,520	$30,240
Group Disability	$0	$0	$0	$0	$0	$0	$0	$0	$0	$0	$0	$0	$0
Group Life	$67	$67	$67	$67	$67	$67	$67	$67	$67	$67	$67	$67	$800
Group Dental	$236	$236	$236	$236	$236	$236	$236	$236	$236	$236	$236	$236	$2,832
Pension Administration	$0	$0	$0	$0	$0	$0	$0	$0	$0	$0	$0	$0	$0
Pension Plan	$0	$0	$0	$0	$0	$0	$0	$0	$0	$0	$0	$0	$0
Profit Sharing	$0	$0	$0	$0	$0	$0	$0	$0	$0	$0	$0	$0	$0
Patient Education Materials	$0	$0	$0	$0	$0	$0	$0	$0	$0	$0	$0	$0	$0
Billing and Collections	$1,653	$2,901	$3,743	$4,175	$4,195	$4,216	$4,238	$4,259	$4,280	$4,301	$4,323	$4,345	$46,629
Bank Charges	$208	$208	$208	$208	$208	$208	$208	$208	$208	$208	$208	$208	$2,500
Continuing Education (staff)	$50	$50	$50	$50	$50	$50	$50	$50	$50	$50	$50	$50	$600
Continuing Education (physician)	$167	$167	$167	$167	$167	$167	$167	$167	$167	$167	$167	$167	$2,000
Computer Depreciation	$0	$0	$0	$0	$0	$0	$0	$0	$0	$0	$0	$0	$0
Asset Depreciation	$319	$319	$319	$319	$319	$319	$319	$319	$319	$319	$319	$319	$3,832

	Month 1	Month 2	Month 3	Month 4	Month 5	Month 6	Month 7	Month 8	Month 9	Month 10	Month 11	Month 12	Totals
Drugs/Immunizations	$1,583	$1,583	$1,583	$1,583	$1,583	$1,583	$1,583	$1,583	$1,583	$1,583	$1,583	$1,583	$19,000
Gifts	$17	$17	$17	$17	$17	$17	$17	$17	$17	$17	$17	$17	$200
Insurance (physician) Malpractice	$210	$210	$210	$210	$210	$210	$210	$210	$210	$210	$210	$210	$2,514
Insurance (other) Malpractice	$0	$0	$0	$0	$0	$0	$0	$0	$0	$0	$0	$0	$0
Laboratory Supplies	$67	$67	$67	$67	$67	$67	$67	$67	$67	$67	$67	$67	$800
Interest Expense (loan)	$0	$0	$0	$0	$0	$0	$0	$0	$0	$0	$0	$0	$0
Licenses and Dues	$250	$250	$250	$250	$250	$250	$250	$250	$250	$250	$250	$250	$3,000
Maintenance and Repair (general)	$475	$475	$475	$475	$475	$475	$475	$475	$475	$475	$475	$475	$5,700
Meals	$29	$29	$29	$29	$29	$29	$29	$29	$29	$29	$29	$29	$350
Meetings/Conferences	$29	$29	$29	$29	$29	$29	$29	$29	$29	$29	$29	$29	$350
Medical Supplies	$808	$808	$808	$808	$808	$808	$808	$808	$808	$808	$808	$808	$9,700
Office Maintenance	$183	$183	$183	$183	$183	$183	$183	$183	$183	$183	$183	$183	$2,200
Office Supplies	$833	$833	$833	$833	$833	$833	$833	$833	$833	$833	$833	$833	$10,000
Postage	$208	$208	$208	$208	$208	$208	$208	$208	$208	$208	$208	$208	$2,500
Professional Services	$750	$750	$750	$750	$750	$750	$750	$750	$750	$750	$750	$750	$9,000
Promotion/Advertising	$333	$333	$333	$333	$333	$333	$333	$333	$333	$333	$333	$333	$4,000
Rental/Leased Equipment	$0	$0	$0	$0	$0	$0	$0	$0	$0	$0	$0	$0	$0

continued

TABLE 7-6 *continued*

Income Statement: Year One

	Month 1	Month 2	Month 3	Month 4	Month 5	Month 6	Month 7	Month 8	Month 9	Month 10	Month 11	Month 12	Totals
Rent (facility)	$2,709	$2,709	$2,709	$2,709	$2,709	$2,709	$2,709	$2,709	$2,709	$2,709	$2,709	$2,709	$32,505
Subscriptions/ Books	$58	$58	$58	$58	$58	$58	$58	$58	$58	$58	$58	$58	$700
Taxes (start-up)	$0	$0	$0	$0	$0	$0	$0	$0	$0	$0	$0	$0	$0
Telephone	$417	$417	$417	$417	$417	$417	$417	$417	$417	$417	$417	$417	$5,000
Travel	$0	$0	$0	$0	$0	$0	$0	$0	$0	$0	$0	$0	$0
Utilities	$1,082	$1,082	$1,082	$1,082	$1,082	$1,082	$1,082	$1,082	$1,082	$1,082	$1,082	$1,082	$12,980
Start-up Expenses	$17,547												$17,547
Total Expenses	$47,375	$31,076	$31,917	$32,349	$32,370	$32,391	$32,412	$32,433	$32,454	$32,476	$32,497	$32,519	$402,268
Net Operating Profit Before Draw and Income Taxes	($26,709)	$5,192	$14,865	$19,834	$20,074	$20,315	$20,558	$20,801	$21,046	$21,292	$21,539	$21,788	$180,596
Physician Draw	$16,667	$16,667	$16,667	$16,667	$16,667	$16,667	$16,667	$16,667	$16,667	$16,667	$16,667	$16,667	$200,000
Physician Payroll Taxes	$1,500	$1,500	$1,500	$1,500	$1,500	$1,500	$1,500	$1,500	$1,500	$1,500	$1,500	$1,500	$18,000
Net Profit Before Income Taxes and Interest Expense	($44,876)	($12,974)	($3,301)	$1,667	$1,907	$2,148	$2,391	$2,634	$2,879	$3,125	$3,373	$3,621	($37,404)
Interest Expense	$0	($478)	($573)	($595)	($580)	($564)	($545)	($525)	($503)	($479)	($453)	($425)	($5,718)
Net Profit After Interest Expense	($44,876)	($13,452)	($3,874)	$1,072	$1,327	$1,585	$1,846	$2,110	$2,377	$2,647	$2,920	$3,196	($43,122)

	Month 13	Month 14	Month 15	Month 16	Month 17	Month 18	Month 19	Month 20	Month 21	Month 22	Month 23	Month 24	Totals
Income													
Professional Fees Collected	$54,578	$54,851	$55,126	$55,401	$55,678	$55,957	$56,236	$56,518	$56,800	$57,084	$57,370	$57,656	$673,256
Other Income	$0	$0	$0	$0	$0	$0	$0	$0	$0	$0	$0	$0	$0
Total Income	$54,578	$54,851	$55,126	$55,401	$55,678	$55,957	$56,236	$56,518	$56,800	$57,084	$57,370	$57,656	$673,256
Expenses													
Staff Salaries	$12,793	$12,793	$12,793	$12,793	$12,793	$12,793	$12,793	$12,793	$12,793	$12,793	$12,793	$12,793	$153,510
Payroll Taxes	$1,151	$1,151	$1,151	$1,151	$1,151	$1,151	$1,151	$1,151	$1,151	$1,151	$1,151	$1,151	$13,815
Insurances													
Group Health	$2,800	$2,800	$2,800	$2,800	$2,800	$2,800	$2,800	$2,800	$2,800	$2,800	$2,800	$2,800	$33,600
Group Disability	$0	$0	$0	$0	$0	$0	$0	$0	$0	$0	$0	$0	$0
Group Life	$70	$70	$70	$70	$70	$70	$70	$70	$70	$70	$70	$70	$840
Group Dental	$255	$255	$255	$255	$255	$255	$255	$255	$255	$255	$255	$255	$3,060
Pension Administration	$0	$0	$0	$0	$0	$0	$0	$0	$0	$0	$0	$0	$0
Pension Plan	$0	$0	$0	$0	$0	$0	$0	$0	$0	$0	$0	$0	$0
Profit Sharing	$0	$0	$0	$0	$0	$0	$0	$0	$0	$0	$0	$0	$0
Patient Education Materials	$0	$0	$0	$0	$0	$0	$0	$0	$0	$0	$0	$0	$0
Billing and Collections	$4,366	$4,388	$4,410	$4,432	$4,454	$4,477	$4,499	$4,521	$4,544	$4,567	$4,590	$4,613	$53,860
Bank Charges	$250	$250	$250	$250	$250	$250	$250	$250	$250	$250	$250	$250	$3,000
Continuing Education (staff)	$53	$53	$53	$53	$53	$53	$53	$53	$53	$53	$53	$53	$630
Continuing Education (physician)	$167	$167	$167	$167	$167	$167	$167	$167	$167	$167	$167	$167	$2,000
Computer Depreciation	$0	$0	$0	$0	$0	$0	$0	$0	$0	$0	$0	$0	$0
Asset Depreciation	$319	$319	$319	$319	$319	$319	$319	$319	$319	$319	$319	$319	$3,832

continued

Financial Management of the Medical Practice

TABLE 7-6 *continued*

Income Statement: Year One

	Month 13	Month 14	Month 15	Month 16	Month 17	Month 18	Month 19	Month 20	Month 21	Month 22	Month 23	Month 24	Totals
Drugs/ Immunizations	$1,663	$1,663	$1,663	$1,663	$1,663	$1,663	$1,663	$1,663	$1,663	$1,663	$1,663	$1,663	$19,950
Gifts	$18	$18	$18	$18	$18	$18	$18	$18	$18	$18	$18	$18	$210
Insurance (physician) Malpractice	$220	$220	$220	$220	$220	$220	$220	$220	$220	$220	$220	$220	$2,640
Insurance (other) Malpractice	$0	$0	$0	$0	$0	$0	$0	$0	$0	$0	$0	$0	$0
Laboratory Fees	$70	$70	$70	$70	$70	$70	$70	$70	$70	$70	$70	$70	$840
Interest Expense (loan)	$0	$0	$0	$0	$0	$0	$0	$0	$0	$0	$0	$0	$0
Licenses and Dues	$263	$263	$263	$263	$263	$263	$263	$263	$263	$263	$263	$263	$3,150
Maintenance and Repair (general)	$499	$499	$499	$499	$499	$499	$499	$499	$499	$499	$499	$499	$5,985
Meals	$31	$31	$31	$31	$31	$31	$31	$31	$31	$31	$31	$31	$368
Meetings/ Conferences	$29	$29	$29	$29	$29	$29	$29	$29	$29	$29	$29	$29	$350
Medical Supplies	$849	$849	$849	$849	$849	$849	$849	$849	$849	$849	$849	$849	$10,185
Office Maintenance	$193	$193	$193	$193	$193	$193	$193	$193	$193	$193	$193	$193	$2,310
Office Supplies	$875	$875	$875	$875	$875	$875	$875	$875	$875	$875	$875	$875	$10,500
Postage	$219	$219	$219	$219	$219	$219	$219	$219	$219	$219	$219	$219	$2,625
Professional Services	$788	$788	$788	$788	$788	$788	$788	$788	$788	$788	$788	$788	$9,450
Promotion/ Advertising	$350	$350	$350	$350	$350	$350	$350	$350	$350	$350	$350	$350	$4,200
Rental/Leased Equipment	$0	$0	$0	$0	$0	$0	$0	$0	$0	$0	$0	$0	$0
Rent (facility)	$2,955	$2,955	$2,955	$2,955	$2,955	$2,955	$2,955	$2,955	$2,955	$2,955	$2,955	$2,955	$35,460

	Month 13	Month 14	Month 15	Month 16	Month 17	Month 18	Month 19	Month 20	Month 21	Month 22	Month 23	Month 24	Totals
Subscriptions/Books	$61	$61	$61	$61	$61	$61	$61	$61	$61	$61	$61	$61	$735
Taxes (start-up)	$0	$0	$0	$0	$0	$0	$0	$0	$0	$0	$0	$0	$0
Telephone	$438	$438	$438	$438	$438	$438	$438	$438	$438	$438	$438	$438	$5,250
Travel	$0	$0	$0	$0	$0	$0	$0	$0	$0	$0	$0	$0	$0
Utilities	$1,136	$1,136	$1,136	$1,136	$1,136	$1,136	$1,136	$1,136	$1,136	$1,136	$1,136	$1,136	$13,629
Start-up Expenses	$0	$0	$0	$0	$0	$0	$0	$0	$0	$0	$0	$0	$0
Total Expenses	$32,877	$32,898	$32,920	$32,942	$32,965	$32,987	$33,009	$33,032	$33,054	$33,077	$33,100	$33,123	$395,984
Net Operating Profit Before Draw and Income Taxes	$21,702	$21,953	$22,205	$22,459	$22,714	$22,970	$23,227	$23,486	$23,746	$24,007	$24,270	$24,534	$277,272
Physician Draw	$17,500	$17,500	$17,500	$17,500	$17,500	$17,500	$17,500	$17,500	$17,500	$17,500	$17,500	$17,500	$210,000
Physician Payroll Taxes	$1,575	$1,575	$1,575	$1,575	$1,575	$1,575	$1,575	$1,575	$1,575	$1,575	$1,575	$1,575	$18,900
Net Profit Before Income Taxes and Interest Expense	$2,627	$2,878	$3,130	$3,384	$3,639	$3,895	$4,152	$4,411	$4,671	$4,932	$5,195	$5,459	$48,372
Interest Expense	($395)	($373)	($349)	($324)	($296)	($266)	($234)	($201)	($165)	($128)	($89)	($47)	($2,868)
Net Profit After Interest Expense	$2,231	$2,505	$2,781	$3,060	$3,343	$3,629	$3,918	$4,210	$4,505	$4,804	$5,106	$5,411	$45,503

SUMMARY

In this chapter, various elements of budgeting and pro forma projections were discussed. Any health care entity, whether a medical practice or other, should use the budget as a basic tool for management and operations. A well-prepared budget is a useful tool to measure performance, even surpassing prior years operating results. It is most useful when prepared by the entire organization and with accountability for meeting its objectives.

The budgeting and pro forma processes are an indispensable part of effective financial management. They can be tedious, yet these are some of the most important functions of the financial manager of the medical practice. Accurate historical operating results are easy to compile and reveal much about the practice. The projections and planning for future performance, however, are more important. They reveal more about where the business is going, than where it has been.

chapter 8

Supplemental Financial Reports

Building on the previously established foundation in earlier chapters, this chapter offers examples of supplemental financial reports that are useful in managing the medical practice. The reports in this chapter vary widely in presentation and appearance. As Chapter 1 affirms, individual practice reporting standards should be established and reflect the specifics and priorities unique to that practice. Chapter 1 introduces some of the basic financial statements, including the income statement, which is a very important report. Many other equally important management reports are illustrated in this chapter. They may be adapted and applied to any practice situation.

DASHBOARD REPORTS

Table 8-1 illustrates a list of *dashboard* reports that alarm the manager when action or reaction needs to occur. The dashboard term is analogous to the dashboard in a vehicle or airplane, and the report can be compared to looking at the gauges on the dashboard to ascertain the performance levels of important functions. Just as the dashboard gauges tell the driver of a need for certain corrective or otherwise reactive actions, so do the red flags that arise in the dashboard report.

A well-run medical practice will have an efficient reporting system to gauge performance. Those reports will be accurate, timely, succinct, and easy to read, so that the manager can draw conclusions and appropriately react. Thus, the capable manager of the practice will be equipped to make beneficial decisions because of accurate and timely dashboard reports.

Just as a driver should regularly check the gauges on to the dashboard for signs of malfunction, so should the practice manager regularly review the dashboard reports. With regular and consistent analysis, the manager and owner of the medical practice can easily monitor results, ascertain both positive and negative trends, and quickly respond. This is the fundamental nature of proper financial management.

Table 8-1 lists a sampling of dashboard reports that are broken down into three major classifications and illustrates the possible reports. Most of these are self-explanatory as to their nature and can be generated from proper practice management information systems. If your information system does not provide a specific report, there is a good chance that the report can be created through

TABLE 8-1

Dashboard Reports

1. Productivity:
    - Visits by provider by site
    - Relative Value Units (RVUs) by provider by site
    - Gross revenue per visit by provider by site
    - Net revenue per visit by provider by site
    - RVUs per visit
    - Hours worked per provider
    - Net revenue per visit
    - Individual payer net charges divided by total net charges (this should be done for all prominent payers)
    - Average charge and reimbursement per patient encounter
    - Number of new patients per full-time equivalent (FTE) provider

2. Financial:
    - Income/expense statement components to budget and previous year by site
    - Staff FTEs by provider
    - Overhead as a percent of net revenue by site/department
    - Collection percentage (gross and net)
    - Days in accounts receivable
    - Accounts receivable percentage by aging category
    - Credit balance summary report
    - Staff payroll plus benefits divided by net revenue
    - Staff hours worked
    - Patient visits
    - Provider compensation as a percentage of net revenue and net collections
    - Average cost per patient including provider salaries and benefits
    - Average cost per patient excluding provider salaries and benefits
    - Departmental expense ratios (ie, total expenses per department divided by total net charges for all CPT codes related to that department)
    - Key elements of overhead relative to net charges and net collections
    - Marketing costs per new patient
    - Time of service collection by site
    - Collections per FTE provider
    - Percentage of accounts receivable over 90 days; percentage over 120 days; percentage over 150 days
    - Payment adjustments by provider, site, and practice/department

3. Operations:
    - Access wait time
    - Telephone abandonment rate
    - Wait time per visit
    - Wait time for return call
    - Accounts worked per billing clerk
    - Missing ticket report
    - Denial and edit report
    - Claim/denial/rejection rate
    - Collection agency collection rate
    - Transcription turnaround
    - Words or lines transcribed per day
    - Accounts worked per day
    - Patient encounters worked per day
    - Payments posted per day

- Billing FTE per provider (excludes data entry)
- Number of appointment slots
- Total appointments divided by total actual appointments
- No-show rate
- Number of new patients per FTE physician
- Number of capitated patients per provider
- Clinical staffing per FTE provider
- Number of health professionals per FTE provider
- Days in back log: charges, payments, and EOBs
- Average number of missing patient encounter forms
- Time of service collection rate
- Patient wait times at time of service
- Patient cancellation rate
- Provider cancellation rate
- Number of referrals by source and/or provider

Source: The Coker Group © 2002.

customization of the data into a reporting tool. The data is already in the system—it merely needs to be organized. In addition, some information systems may be able to be migrated into a spreadsheet program, such as MS Excel, Lotus Notes, or MS Access. As a final alternative (although not recommended unless there are no other options), the spreadsheet can be completed by dropping (or dumping) the data that is within the information system to paper, then converting it into the spreadsheet.

Most of the reports in Table 8-1 have been discussed at various places within this book. We will consider and illustrate examples of many of these in the remainder of this chapter.

FLASH REPORTS

The following examples, which are called *flash reports*, illustrate basic summary data for the entire practice. Flash reports are overall summaries of practice performance that may be completed at regular, defined intervals (ie, at least monthly) and presented for management review. These reports should be given to each physician (whether physician-owned or not) and used for establishing key discussion points to be addressed during management meetings. They can also be useful for evaluating individual performance, if the same information is provided on an individual physician/provider basis, which is a possibility.

The information on the flash reports is basic, yet informative. This is relative to the overall performance, using key data such as gross charges, net charges, net collections, overhead expense, number of patients, number of new patients, and so on. All non-financial personnel, including physician-owners, can readily understand these flash reports, which will benefit their future performance.

Flash reports should be used on a monthly basis, with encouragement given to the physicians (certainly the physician-owners) to carry these reports with them as a continual reminder of their past

TABLE 8-2

Sample Monthly Flash Report

	Fiscal Year-to-Date			Year-to-Date		
Provider Performance	**Practice Totals**	**Per FTE Provider**	**Benchmarking Comparison**	**Practice Totals**	**Per FTE Provider**	**Benchmarking Comparison**
Provider gross charges	$90,000	$30,000	$35,000	$285,000	$95,000	$105,000
Provider compensation	$30,000	$10,000	$11,000	$90,000	$30,000	$33,000
Ambulatory encounters	40	13	14	120	40	42
Accounts Receivable Management and Collections Programs	**Practice**	**Comparison**		**Financial Snapshot**	**Practice**	**Per FTE Physician**
Months FFS charges in A/R	3.6	3.2		Gross patient revenue	$285,000	$95,000
% of A/R over 120 days	20%	18%		**Total net revenue**	$190,100	$63,367
A/R per FTE physician	$325,000	$295,000		Total Expenses	$86,000	$28,667
Net collection percentage	91%	95%		EBITDA	$104,100	$34,700
MD Comp. as % of Net Production	**Practice**	**Comparison**				
MD comp. as a % of net production	55%	53%				
Expenses as a % of Net Revenue	**Practice**	**Comparison**				
Physician compensation	45%	48%				
Physician benefits	10%	10%				
Mid-level provider compensation	4%	4%				
Mid-level provider benefits	1%	1%				
Support staff costs	20%	21%				
Support staff benefits	3%	3%				
Supplies	1.5%	2%				
Insurance	3%	3.5%				
Square footage per physicians	TBD	TBD				

Source: The Coker Group © 2002.

T A B L E 8-3

Sample Monthly Flash Report

	Goal	Current Month	Previous Month	YTD
Billings				
Adjustments				
Collections Percentage (Fee-for-service cash collections/fee-for-service charges)				
Total Accounts Ratio (Total nonphysician expenses + average monthly billings)				
New Patients				
Total New Patients				
Expense Ratio (Total nonphysician expenses + total net charges)				
Profit <loss> (cash basis) (Collections minus expenses)				
Net Income Percentage (Total net revenue + collections				

Source: The Coker Group © 2002.

and future performance expectations. Tables 8-2, 8-3, and 8-4 are examples of monthly flash reports.

Note that a *Goal* column has been placed to the left of the *Current Month, Previous Month,* and *Year-To-Date (YTD)* results. It is important to reflect this Goal or perhaps better stated, *Budgeted Total,* in the summary report. In most cases, this column should be used as a measurement of the operating results for the *Current Month*. While it is good to know historical information as a comparison (ie, *Previous Month*), it is more significant to compare the *Current Month* operations against the *budget* or *goal* amount.

DETAILED REPORTS

The following are a detailed assortment of management report examples compiled from an operating practice, which includes the dynamics of outpatient, inpatient, procedural activity, and some ancillary services. It includes a practice with a number of providers (mostly physicians) and multiple locations. It considers a variety of payers and, within the provider base, includes numerous variables as to length of tenure with the practice and in the overall practice of medicine, hours worked per week/year, and the general style of practice within the various providers. The schedules that are illustrated include both traditional spreadsheet summary data as well as more visual graphic illustrations. In many instances, the

TABLE 8-4

Sample Monthly Flash Report

	Month:	_____
Total Charges		_____
Adjustments		_____
Net Charges		_____
Total Receipts		_____
Adjustments		_____
Total Patients Seen		_____
Total New Patients Seen		_____
Daily Average		_____
Collection Ratio		_____
Accounts Receivable		_____
Average Per Patient Charge		_____
Average Per Patient Cost		_____
Total Monthly Expenses		_____
Net Income		_____

Source: The Coker Group © 2002.

graphic illustration follows and/or mirrors the previous spreadsheet. This is an informative way to present financial information. First, list it in a data formatted spreadsheet; then follow this with a more visual illustration through an appropriate graph or chart. Most information systems and/or other software packages can easily derive both types of financial performance schedules/illustrations. Thus, the _package_ of information is more readily accepted and absorbed by the generalist (ie, usually the practice manager and physician-owners).

The following tables consider various areas of performance within the practice. They can also be related to the Dashboard Reports that were previously explained.

Productivity Reports

Within productivity, performance has been reviewed throughout the past five years, which includes a breakdown between office and hospital. Table 8-5 illustrates the breakdown.

Figure 8-1 illustrates how patient encounters have varied throughout the historical period, again breaking these down by office visits, hospital visits, and new patients.

In Table 8-6, each provider's productivity is then compared from one year to the next throughout the five-year period, with that productivity being measured on patient encounters.

Another way to consider productivity is the relativity of patient days to days worked. This is illustrated via graph in Figure 8-2.

Similar information can be summarized in a more traditional spreadsheet format (Table 8-7), wherein the days worked can be compared to the visits/patient encounters and those then allocated on a per day basis for each provider.

Table 8-8 offers much insight into each physician/provider's true productivity. While one physician might have more cumulative

TABLE 8-5

Office/Hospital Breakdown

	1997	**1998**	**1999**	**2000**	**2001**
Office	28,863	35,114	35,753	32,652	38,760
Hospital	2,153	2,004	1,690	1,555	1,051
Total	**31,016**	**37,118**	**37,443**	**34,207**	**39,811**
Provider FTE	8.5	11.8	11.5	9.8	11.1
Per Provider	3,649	3,159	3,256	3,480	3,587
New Patients	3,433	2,877	2,774	1,535	3,359

- ■ Total patient encounters up by 16%
- ■ Hospital encounters up by 50%
- ■ Per provider encounters up by 3%
- ■ New patient encounters up by 110%

Source: The Coker Group © 2002.

FIGURE 8-1

Patient Encounters

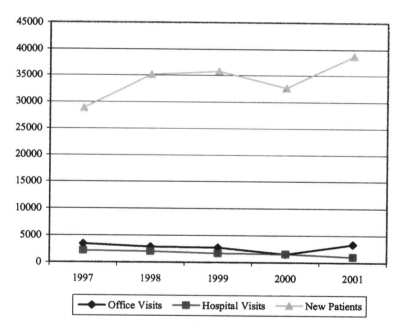

Source: The Coker Group © 2002.

patient encounters, if he or she works a greater number of days, the average patient encounters per day may be much lower than his/her peers, or even lower than acceptable benchmarks. This report, as depicted in Table 8-7, attempts to peel back the layers to get to the actual picture of performance.

Other measurements of productivity include new patients as allocated to each provider (Table 8-8) and the overall breakdown of the types of visits within each physician's practice (ie, in-office patient encounters, hospital encounters, mid-level support encounters, employee physicals) (Table 8-9).

TABLE 8-6

Productivity

Physician	1997	1998	1999	2000	2001
A	3,724	3,410	3,445	3,353	3,514
B	3,951	3,220	2,590	2,963	2,838
C	4,032	3,573	3,139	3,647	3,494
D	3,212	2,786	2,592	2,733	2,623
E	1,497	3,411	4,273	4,255	4,323
F	2,348	3,753	3,426	3,926	3,486
G		3,853	3,570	3,808	3,692
H		579	3,191	3,542	3,736
I					4,223
J					3,736
K					2,753
L					1,155
Total	18,764	24,585	26,226	28,227	39,573

Source: The Coker Group © 2002.

FIGURE 8-2

Patient Visits versus Days Worked

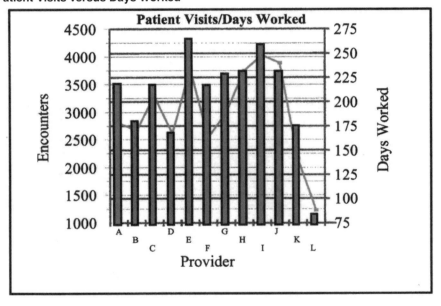

Source: The Coker Group © 2002.

Coding trends can be viewed under the broad definition of productivity. These reports normally focus on the various levels of *evaluation and management* (E&M) codes. A practice with various providers will have different styles of coding, with each provider having a unique style. Every practice should have a compliance program to monitor coding practices and to educate the physicians on coding and documentation requirements. Table 8-10 illustrates each physician's level of coding, revealing the different approaches to coding and, more importantly, indicating a need for further education/assistance to enhance. Most physicians have a tendency to undercode for the level of services performed. Table 8-10 clearly

TABLE 8-7

Patient Visits versus Days Worked

Physician	Days Worked	Visits			Visits per Day		
		Office	Hospital	Total	Office	Hospital	Total
A	178	3,466	48	3,514	19.5	0.3	19.7
B	170	2,832	6	2,838	16.7	0.0	16.7
C	206	3,256	238	3,494	15.8	1.2	17.0
D	167	2,535	88	2,623	15.2	0.5	15.7
E	234	4,203	120	4,323	18.0	0.5	18.5
F	162.5	3,491	0	3,486	21.5		21.5
G	189	3,563	129	3,692	18.9	0.7	19.5
H	232	3,527	209	3,736	15.2	0.9	16.1
I	248	4,102	121	4,223	16.5	0.5	17.0
J	240	3,670	69	3,739	15.3	0.3	15.6
K	141	2,753	0	2,753	19.5		19.5
L	88	1,133	22	1,155	12.9	0.3	13.1
Resident		230	0	230			
Total	**2,271**	**38,760**	**1,051**	**39,811**	**17.1**	**0.5**	**17.5**

Source: The Coker Group © 2002.

TABLE 8-8

New Patients

#	Physician	# New Patients
1	A	233
2	B	14
3	C	201
11	D	33
14	E	202
15	F	163
16	G	82
19	H	177
22	I	985
24	J	828
25	K	127
27	L	307
	Resident	7
	All Other	
	Total	3,359

Source: The Coker Group © 2002.

illustrates a trend of a particular provider to undercode. When undercoding like such is seen, management should take the appropriate steps to work with that physician/provider through either a detailed chart audit or simply through coding education. The inherent benefit of such an analysis may be the legitimate increase of revenue for that provider and the entire practice.

TABLE 8-9

Visit Types

Physician	In office Enc	Hospital Enc	Mid Level	Employed Physician	Total
A	3,466	48	469	169	4,152
B	2,832	6	544	132	3,514
C	3,256	238	976	311	4,781
D	2,535	88	1,367	318	4,308
E	4,203	120	1,044	221	5,588
F	3,491	0	494	139	4,124
G	3,563	129	757	189	4,638
H	3,527	209	450	-600	3,586
I	4,102	121	222	-600	3,845
J	3,670	69	74	-279	3,534
K	2,753	0	0	0	2,753
L	1,133		0	0	1,155
Resident	230	22			230
Total	**38,760**	**1,051**	**6,397**	**0**	**46,208**

Source: The Coker Group © 2002.

TABLE 8-10

Coding Variances Among Physicians

Physician	Level 1	Level 2	Level 3	Level 4	Level 5
A	0.00%	4.85%	60.27%	15.32%	19.56%
B	0.11%	7.32%	35.05%	46.70%	10.82%
C	0.00%	2.25%	50.81%	28.52%	18.42%
D	0.04%	0.08%	50.32%	6.14%	43.42%
E	0.02%	1.39%	48.26%	20.69%	29.64%
F	0.03%	20.83%	69.24%	9.58%	0.32%
G	0.00%	0.57%	42.42%	37.61%	19.39%
H	0.00%	0.64%	69.46%	9.42%	20.49%
I	0.00%	1.90%	65.72%	22.79%	9.58%
J	0.00%	0.25%	19.88%	57.00%	22.88%
K	0.04%	16.31%	76.28%	7.37%	0.00%
L	0.00%	0.00%	49.82%	18.49%	31.24%
Resident	—	—	—	—	—
All Other	9.21%	20.61%	66.23%	3.51%	0.44%
Total	**0.08%**	**4.99%**	**55.08%**	**24.53%**	**15.32%**

Source: The Coker Group © 2002.

Coding comparisons can illustrate how physicians/providers vary from each other at the various levels of coding.

Coding variances from prior years can also be illustrated, as shown by Table 8-11.

Provider physician productivity can also be measured based on the type of services that are provided. Table 8-12 illustrates various types of provided services, including outpatient visits, consultations, hospitals, radiology, lab, echocardiogram, and other ancillaries, venipuncture, and other activities. It provides a succinct, informative

TABLE 8-11

Coding Variances From Prior Years

Physician	Level 1	Level 2	Level 3	Level 4	Level 5
A		4.48%	4.11%	-2.84%	-2.74%
B	-0.04%	0.80%	11.41%	-4.93%	-7.25%
C		-3.96%	-6.95%	8.45%	2.46%
D	-0.08%	-0.15%	1.23%		-1.00%
E	0.02%	0.46%	4.18%	1.28%	-5.94%
F	-0.05%	4.91%	5.77%	-10.03%	-0.60%
G		-0.68%	-6.55%	5.46%	1.77%
H		-83.36%	-5.48%	1.37%	4.32%
I		1.90%	65.72%	22.79%	9.58%
J		0.25%	19.88%	57.00%	22.88%
K		-61.51%	54.92%	6.55%	
L			49.82%	18.49%	31.24%
Resident					
All Other	9.21%	20.61%	0.52%	-30.78%	0.44%
Total	**0.05%**	**-1.74%**	**0.77%**	**3.35%**	**-2.43%**

Source: The Coker Group © 2002.

Note: Blank entry indicates no such entry recorded.

TABLE 8-12

Services Provided

Physician	OV	Consult	Hospital	Radiology	Lab	Echo/U/s	Skin/Flex Venipuncture	Resp/Join Insurance	Immunization
A	$187,250	$399	$3,940	$25,239	$67,780	$10,529	$5,281	$18,787	$2,465
B	$138,136	$91	$2,553	$11,442	$42,482	$2,830	$10,238	$10,022	$2,107
C	$171,734		$18,031	$29,496	$43,030	$12,471	$7,100	$18,021	$4,765
D	$166,204	$160	$7,121	$46,392	$62,579	$12,602	$4,541	$14,168	$5,661
E	$240,887	$1,003	$13,145	$42,363	$46,119	$29,049	$12,687	$25,714	$18,889
F	$123,224			$6,127	$16,777		$6,392	$6,206	$2,421
G	$193,508	$2,434	$10,253	$39,241	$39,242	$14,358	$9,252	$18,642	$3,347
H	$161,722	$989	$18,865	$30,582	$35,432	$14,024	$10,017	$16,236	$7,639
I	$177,497	$315	$6,810	$12,308	$20,793	$9,142	$1,917	$4,508	$4,430
J	$198,503		$5,765	$1,367	$35,028	$13,088	$7,975	$4,173	$3,139
K	$49,257		$1,152	$2,845	$6,418	$561	$1,089	$1,683	$354
L	$97,730			$314	$8,551	$863	$4,777	$3,997	$1,231
Total	$1,924,128	$5,391	$87,916	$263,777	$428,659	$120,804	$82,471	$143,095	$57,356

Source: The Coker Group © 2002.

Note: Blank entry indicates no such entry recorded.

report of the sources of revenue by the provider physician. This same information can also then be converted to percentages, as shown is Table 8-13.

Productivity can be measured for certain ancillary services, as is illustrated in Table 8-14 by the number of bone density reviews in that particular schedule.

TABLE 8-13

Services Provided (Percentages)

Physician	OV	Consult	Hospital	Radiology	Lab	Echo/U/s	Skin/Flex Venipuncture	Resp/Join Insurance	Immunization
A	58.21%	0.12%	1.22%	7.85%	21.07%	3.27%	1.64%	5.84%	0.77%
B	62.82%	0.04%	1.16%	5.20%	19.32%	1.29%	4.66%	4.56%	0.96%
C	56.37%	0.00%	5.92%	9.68%	14.12%	4.09%	2.33%	5.92%	1.56%
D	52.03%	0.05%	2.23%	14.52%	19.59%	3.95%	1.42%	4.44%	1.77%
E	56.04%	0.23%	3.06%	9.86%	10.73%	6.76%	2.95%	5.98%	4.39%
F	76.47%	0.00%	0.00%	3.80%	10.41%	0.00%	3.97%	3.85%	1.50%
G	58.59%	0.74%	3.10%	11.88%	11.88%	4.35%	2.80%	5.64%	1.01%
H	54.73%	0.33%	6.38%	10.35%	11.99%	4.75%	3.39%	5.49%	2.59%
I	74.67%	0.13%	2.86%	5.18%	8.75%	3.85%	0.81%	1.90%	1.86%
J	73.78%	0.00%	2.14%	0.51%	13.02%	4.86%	2.96%	1.55%	1.17%
K	77.74%	0.00%	1.82%	4.49%	10.13%	0.89%	1.72%	2.66%	0.56%
L	83.20%	0.00%	0.00%	0.27%	7.28%	0.73%	4.07%	3.40%	1.05%
Total	**61.80%**	**0.17%**	**2.82%**	**8.47%**	**13.77%**	**3.88%**	**2.65%**	**4.60%**	**1.84%**

Source: The Coker Group © 2002.

TABLE 8-14

Ancillary Services

#	Physician	# Bone Density Reviews
1	A	120
2	B	73
3	C	166
11	D	283
14	E	266
15	F	1
16	G	184
19	H	139
22	I	86
24	J	92
25	K	0
27	L	26
	All Other	0
	Total	**1,436**

Source: The Coker Group © 2002.

Revenue Reports

On an overall basis, the practice can illustrate its revenue and other key data pertaining to the generation of fees. Medical practices, unfortunately, do not collect full charges due to the dynamics of managed care and government reimbursement that demand huge discounts. It is important to monitor this information and to convert it to ratios. Table 8-15 illustrates comparative charges, payments, and collection ratios of its patient encounters during the past five years.

TABLE 8-15

Comparative Charges, Payments, and Collection Ratios

Year	Encounters	Charges	Payments	Collection Ratio	Charges/Pt	Payments/Pt
1996	31,016	$3,866,617	$2,470,604	63.90%	$124.67	$79.66
1997	37,118	$4,536,092	$3,006,005	66.27%	$122.21	$80.99
1998	37,443	$4,687,093	$3,210,263	68.49%	$125.18	$85.74
1999	34,207	$4,427,097	$3,095,546	69.92%	$129.42	$90.49
2000	39,811	$5,320,590	$3,782,561	71.09%	$133.65	$95.01

Source: The Coker Group © 2002.

FIGURE 8-3

Charges/Payments by Encounter

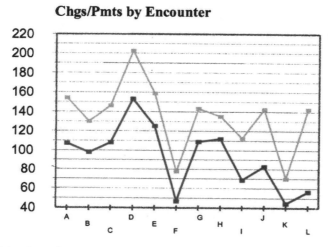

Source: The Coker Group © 2002.

Table 8-15 is short, easy to understand, and should be an effective tool in making decisions. (While we have illustrated most of these schedules on a yearly basis, similar schedules could be completed on a monthly basis within each year. Instead of the schedule illustrating details during the prior five years, it could be prepared for and as of the end of each month within a given year.)

Charges and payments by patient encounter can also be graphically illustrated, as in Figure 8-3.

Charges and payments by provider, both in dollars and graphic form, should also be included, as illustrated in Table 8-16. The variances from the prior year should be likewise considered.

Revenue should be considered on a by-payer basis. Table 8-17 illustrates collection ratios by payer, concisely presented on one simple schedule. Breaking this down further, dollars per patient encounter by payer can be informative. Comparing these totals to the prior-year's collection ratio and dollars per patient encounter for each payer, as shown in Table 8-18, also illustrates how changes in managed care contracts have affected each payer's status.

TABLE 8-16

Charges and Payments by Provider

Physician	Charges	Payments	Adjustments	Charges/ Encounter	Payments/ Encounter	Adjustments/ Encounter
A	$540,516	$377,557	($177,408)	$153.82	$107.44	($50.49)
B	$368,512	$277,898	($106,354)	$129.85	$97.92	($37.47)
C	$510,199	$377,487	($142,774)	$146.02	$108.04	($40.86)
D	$530,926	$401,472	($142,584)	$202.41	$153.06	($54.36)
E	$685,697	$541,095	($174,806)	$158.62	$125.17	($40.44)
F	$270,458	$163,430	($126,583)	$77.58	$46.88	($36.31)
G	$528,514	$403,118	($151,010)	$143.15	$109.19	($40.90)
H	$504,815	$418,612	($107,130)	$135.12	$112.05	($28.68)
I	$474,386	$289,214	($133,486)	$112.33	$68.49	($31.61)
J	$532,526	$308,761	($171,830)	$142.54	$82.64	($45.99)
K	$192,382	$122,503	($81,283)	$69.88	$44.50	($29.53)
L	$164,404	$65,170	($45,837)	$142.34	$56.42	($39.69)
Total	$5,303,335	$3,746,317	($1,561,085)	$134.01	$94.67	($39.45)

Source: The Coker Group © 2002.

TABLE 8-17

Collection Ratios by Payer

Plan	2001 Encounters	2001 Collection Ratio	2000 Collection Ratio	Difference
Cigna HMO	4,757	93.77%	103.00%	-9.23%
Aetna Cap	4,607	93.16%	98.10%	-4.94%
Cigna Senior	159	81.39%	65.90%	15.49%
Private Pay	428	81.34%	100.10%	-18.76%
MPMP	3,179	78.53%	65.00%	13.53%
Xmar	146	77.96%	79.40%	-1.44%
PHCS	575	74.25%	88.20%	-13.95%
United Healthcare	4,497	74.15%	64.80%	9.35%
Community Care Network	738	74.06%	78.80%	-4.74%
Humana	2,298	72.96%	70.10%	2.86%
Railroad Medicare	116	72.16%	61.00%	11.16%
Foundation for Medical Care	1,237	71.71%	75.40%	-3.69%
No Insurance	957	70.95%	81.70%	-10.75%
Jones	827	70.53%		
XYZ Street	184	70.05%	93.50%	-23.45%
One Health Plan	513	70.01%	76.90%	-6.89%
Aetna	1,121	68.88%	73.40%	-4.52%
Medicare	7,780	60.50%	59.30%	1.20%
Champus	77	59.04%	70.70%	-11.66%
X Management	680	58.28%	57.30%	0.98%
BC/BS	3,482	57.25%	59.40%	-2.15%
Cigna	724	53.43%	70.10%	-16.67%
First Health	58	43.82%		
Total	39,140	71.25%	70.00%	1.25%

Source: The Coker Group © 2002.

TABLE 8-18

Dollars per Patient Encounter

Plan	Encounters	2001 $/Encounter	2000 $/Encounter	Difference
Cigna Senior	159	$285.92	$65.80	$220.12
Private Pay	428	$177.28	$218.90	-$41.62
Community Care Network	738	$141.09	$123.60	$17.49
Foundation for Medical Care	1,237	$135.69	$128.50	$7.19
XYZ Street	184	$122.77	$17.90	$104.87
Champus	77	$121.05	$108.10	$12.95
Xmar	146	$117.38	$117.80	-$0.42
BC/BS	3,482	$113.94	$119.90	-$5.96
Medicare	7,780	$104.93	$99.00	$5.93
MPMP	3,179	$102.94	$122.10	-$19.16
Railroad Medicare	116	$102.52	$128.00	-$25.48
X Management	680	$93.87	$82.70	$11.17
PHCS	575	$93.11	$108.50	-$15.39
Jones	827	$90.57	—	NC
Cigna	724	$88.55	$73.30	$15.25
One Health Plan	513	$84.57	$91.40	-$6.83
Aetna Cap	4,607	$83.41	$77.50	$5.91
Cigna HMO	4,757	$78.36	$93.10	-$14.74
United Healthcare	4,497	$78.20	$72.00	$6.20
Humana	2,298	$77.91	$74.90	$3.01
Aetna	1,121	$67.85	$53.00	$14.85
Health First	58	$59.12	—	NC
No Insurance	957	$53.31	$65.20	-$11.89
Total	39,140	$94.89	$90.50	$4.39

Source: The Coker Group © 2002.

NC = not comparable.

Payer Analysis

A review of a payer analysis within the practice (Table 8-19) is important. If capitation exists, this should be illustrated among the major capitated payers. Total dollars and the relative percent that each capitated payer has to the total capitated dollars should be considered. Payments per patient encounter and collection ratios are also important.

Likewise, it is important to consider total capitation by physician on the payer analysis. Table 8-20 helps to illustrate on a per physician basis not only where the capitated dollars are being realized, but the degree of collectability on those dollars within each provider. This enables a better understanding and management of the physicians, including improved administration of their compensation.

Also within the payer analysis, a schedule may consider an illustration of a percent of revenue by provider by plan, which is very informative in developing go-forward strategies for managed care. This can vary from one provider to another, as is illustrated in Table 8-21. Decisions must be made for how best to interpret this information and then develop a strategy for the practice's managed care initiatives.

TABLE 8-19

Payer Analysis

Year	Cigna	Aetna	HPHP	Total	% Rev/Cap
1996	$354,411	$98,901		$453,312	18.4%
1997	$598,531	$118,126	$57,161	$773,818	25.7%
1998	$552,332	$50,755	$168,721	$771,808	27.2%
1999	$344,272	$189,812		$534,084	17.3%
2000	$372,749	$384,279		$757,028	20.0%

Year	Cigna	Aetna	Cigna	Aetna
1996	$82	$83	84.73%	91.37%
1997	$93	$78	103.75%	78.78%
1998	$85	$73	95.58%	81.17%
1999	$88	$85	99.22%	91.83%
2000	$78	$83	93.77%	93.16%

Source: The Coker Group © 2002.

TABLE 8-20

Total Capitation by Physician

#	Physician	Charges	Payments	Collection Ratio	Payments/Encounter
1	A	$43,317	$54,727	126.34%	$102.10
2	B	$56,789	$62,056	109.27%	$95.77
3	C	$72,622	$73,869	101.72%	$101.61
11	D	$56,268	$91,284	162.23%	$188.60
14	E	$82,946	$114,277	137.77%	$156.33
15	F	$70,303	$10,710	15.23%	$11.19
16	G	$83,022	$82,907	99.86%	$105.61
19	H	$94,710	$131,527	138.87%	$135.88
22	I	$110,680	$74,120	66.97%	$57.19
24	J	$72,968	$34,912	47.85%	$38.49
25	K	$46,813	$7,109	15.19%	$10.41
27	L				
	All Other	$4,185	$761	18.18%	$9.63
	Total	**$794,623**	**$738,259**	**92.91%**	**$82.02**

Source: The Coker Group © 2002.

Expense Analysis

Obviously, expenses should be considered in any reporting process for the practice. These may be broken down in greater detail than what is illustrated in these schedules. However, on a comparative basis, it is important to summarize and separate between provider and nonprovider costs (Table 8-22). Practice overhead is defined by those costs that are nonprovider related. The assumption is that, in a private practice, all monies left over after nonprovider expenses are paid go to the physician-owners. Therefore, to ascertain a true

TABLE 8-21

Percent of Revenue by Provider by Plan

	A	B	C	D	E	G	H	I	J	L
Medicare	31.5%	34.8%	27.7%	25.3%	18.7%	23.5%	14.4%	12.9%	17.3%	20.0%
Blue Cross	15.9%	8.0%	9.5%	11.2%	8.5%	7.1%	10.5%	10.4%	13.0%	11.1%
United Healthcare	11.0%	11.9%	16.2%	15.0%	21.7%	20.5%	16.9%	18.0%	20.4%	18.1%
Cigna	7.7%	13.6%	12.7%	14.6%	13.2%	16.7%	17.8%	15.5%	6.5%	6.7%
Aetna	11.1%	13.6%	12.6%	12.4%	13.6%	7.7%	19.1%	15.8%	9.8%	7.8%
Foundation for Medical Care	4.1%	3.8%	3.5%	4.6%	3.2%	6.0%	4.2%	4.1%	5.8%	5.8%
X Management	2.3%	0.4%	0.5%	1.5%	3.4%	0.7%	1.5%	1.5%	0.7%	4.3%
XYZ Health Plan	0.8%	1.5%	2.4%	1.8%	2.7%	2.4%	1.3%	2.1%	1.5%	2.7%
CCN	3.8%	1.7%	1.6%	2.5%	2.3%	2.5%	2.3%	3.8%	4.3%	2.7%
One Health Plan	1.0%	0.3%	0.5%	0.6%	1.2%	1.2%	0.6%	2.5%	2.6%	1.9%
Private Pay	1.9%	2.6%	1.8%	2.7%	2.5%	2.0%	0.8%	1.4%	2.1%	0.8%
Humana	4.1%	2.9%	5.3%	3.3%	4.9%	3.8%	5.0%	6.3%	7.3%	8.0%
PHCS	1.1%	0.8%	1.5%	1.2%	1.3%	1.4%	1.2%	1.5%	2.4%	2.7%
No Insurance	1.5%	1.4%	0.5%	1.0%	0.7%	1.5%	0.8%	1.8%	1.8%	5.0%

Source: The Coker Group © 2002.

TABLE 8-22

Provider versus Nonprovider Costs

	Nonprovider Cost	% of Revenue	Cost/ Encounter	Revenue Per Encounter	Net to Providers
1996	$1,343,756	60.70%	$51.80	$85.30	$33.50
1997	$1,499,569	59.10%	$48.30	$81.80	$33.50
1998	$1,878,078	60.70%	$50.60	$83.40	$32.80
1999	$1,987,515	60.80%	$53.18	$87.40	$34.22
2000	$1,941,149	62.80%	$56.75	$90.31	$33.56
2001	$2,156,169	56.92%	$54.16	$95.16	$41.00

Source: The Coker Group © 2002.

operating overhead rate, such nonprovider costs should be separately analyzed.

More specific departmental costs can also be considered. Table 8-23 illustrates lab and X-ray expense as opposed to their revenues and resultant profit.

Expense analysis can also be more specifically broken down, such as transcription. Practices with several providers usually vary significantly in transcription time based upon the amount of dictation. Such expenses can be monitored and illustrated on a per provider basis, as shown in Table 8-24. This table shows the cost per patient encounter for transcription in comparison to the prior year. This is a very useful tool to better manage the physicians and also, where appropriate, to implement as a component of their compensation structure (ie, those that use more transcription services and entail greater costs may be allocated more expense). These can also be illustrated on a payer basis, as illustrated in Figure 8-4.

TABLE 8-23

Specific Expenses

	Revenues	% of Total Revenue	Expense	Profit	Overhead
	Lab				
1998	$444,535	14.79%	$217,954	$226,581	49.03%
1999	$456,515	14.22%	$215,836	$240,679	47.28%
2000	$464,695	15.01%	$243,253	$221,442	52.35%
2001	$428,659	11.33%	$246,071	$182,588	57.40%
	X-ray				
1998	$59,631	1.98%	$48,000	$11,631	80.50%
1999	$73,580	2.29%	$55,514	$18,066	75.45%
2000	$90,546	2.93%	$58,773	$31,773	64.91%
2001	$263,777	6.97%	$79,843	$183,934	30.27%

Source: The Coker Group © 2002.

TABLE 8-24

Expenses per Provider

Physician	Trans Costs	2001 Cost/Enc	2000 Cost/Enc
A	$6,622	$1.88	$2.29
B	$7,213	$2.54	$2.30
C	$10,698	$3.06	$2.41
D	$8,567	$3.27	$2.65
E	$10,380	$2.40	$2.58
F	$9,454	$2.71	$3.42
G	$16,255	$4.40	$3.54
H	$11,312	$3.03	$2.62
I	$14,476	$3.43	NA
J	$16,093	$4.31	NA
K	$9,109	$3.31	$4.97
L	$5,595	$4.84	NA
Total	$125,774	$3.18	$3.01

Source: The Coker Group © 2002.

NA = not applicable; not employed in prior year.

Accounts Receivable Analysis

Other important reports, such as examples of accounts receivable analysis, can be stated in terms of number of days and broken down by payer, as illustrated in Table 8-25.

These schedules inform and help determine accounts receivable problems and opportunities.

Personal Physician Overhead Analysis

On an overall basis, schedules can be derived that illustrate overhead in a broader sense, on a per physician basis. Much of the

FIGURE 8-4

Expenses per Payer

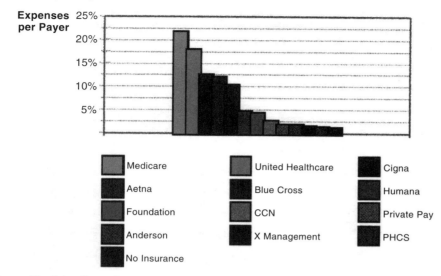

Source: The Coker Group © 2002.

TABLE 8-25

Accounts Receivable Analysis

DATE	
Gross Accounts Receivable	$500,000
Divided by: Gross FFS charges last three months	700,000
Times: Number of days last three months	90.0
Equals: Days of Gross Revenue A/R	64.29
Net accounts receivable	$300,000
Divided by: Net FFS charges last three months	525,000
Times: Number of days last three months	90.0
Equals: Days of Net Revenue in A/R	**51.43**
Date	
Gross Accounts Receivable	$500,000
Divided by: Gross FFS charges	700,000
Times: Three	0.3
Equals: Months Gross FFS Charges in A/R	**2.14**
Comparison (Benchmark)	TBD
A/R Aging	
Current	$150,000
31–60 days	175,000
61–90 days	50,000
91–120 days	25,000
121–150 days	20,000
Over 150 days	10,000
	$500,000

continued

TABLE 8-25 *continued*

Accounts Receivable Analysis

PERCENTAGE OF A/R OVER 120 DAYS	20.0%
Comparison (Benchmark)	TBD
A/R PER FTE PHYSICIAN	**$166,667**
Comparison (Benchmark)	TBD

Source: The Coker Group © 2002.

TABLE 8-26

Per Physician Overhead Analysis

Physician	Days Worked	Total Encounters	Encounter/ Day	Pay	2001 Pay/Day	2001 Pay/ Encounter	2000 Pay/Day	2000 Pay/ Encounter
A	178.0	3,514	19.74	$142,321	$799.56	$40.50	$694.00	$35.40
B	170.0	2,838	16.69	$77,207	$454.16	$27.20	$405.00	$23.10
C	206.0	3,494	16.96	$171,734	$833.66	$49.15	$666.00	$36.70
D	167.0	2,623	15.71	$150,751	$902.70	$57.47	$626.00	$40.10
E	234.0	4,323	18.47	$266,975	$1,140.92	$61.76	$897.00	$47.30
F	162.5	3,486	21.45	$98,000	$603.08	$28.11	$358.00	$16.80
G	189.0	3,692	19.53	$170,562	$902.44	$46.20	$651.00	$32.70
H	232.0	3,736	16.10	$186,041	$801.90	$49.80	$598.00	$39.40
I	248.0	4,223	17.03	$141,842	$571.94	$33.59	NA	NA
J	240.0	3,736	15.57	$148,263	$617.76	$39.68	NA	NA
K	141.0	2,753	19.52	$115,029	$815.80	$41.78	NA	NA
L	88.0	1,155	13.13	$74,238	$843.60	$64.28	NA	NA
Total	2255.5	39,573	17.55	$1,742,963	$772.76	$44.04	$684.29	$39.16

Source: The Coker Group © 2002.

NA = not applicable; not employed in prior year.

information that is illustrated in the previous schedules and charts is summarized and provides informative, yet succinct, indicators of performance. This is then related to the individual physician's compensation in terms of both (1) total pay and compensation per day per patient encounter and (2) totals compared to the prior year, as illustrated in Table 8-26.

The personal physician overhead analysis can also be considered based upon the utilization of mid-level extenders and how this affects their performance and the overhead that they consume, as shown in Table 8-27.

SUMMARY

Summary schedules are essential in interpreting financial performance. Formal financial statements (ie, income statement, balance sheets, statement of changes in financial position) are important and necessary; however, more detailed and specific issue-directed summaries facilitate beneficial management decisions. Each practice should formulate its reports specific to the practice,

TABLE 8-27

Effect of Mid-Level Extenders

Physician	Collections	Extender Util	Net Collection	Pay	2001 Overhead	2000 Overhead
A	$377,540	122	$370,830	$142,321	61.62%	66.27%
B	$277,816	197	$266,981	$77,207	71.08%	75.32%
C	$377,216	373	$356,701	$171,734	51.85%	57.16%
D	$401,686	383	$380,621	$150,751	60.39%	67.71%
E	$540,414	305	$523,639	$266,975	49.02%	56.32%
G	$403,072	185	$392,897	$170,562	56.59%	64.69%
H	$418,384	303	$401,719	$186,041	53.69%	
Total	$2,796,128	1868	$2,693,388	$1,165,591	56.72%	

Source: The Coker Group © 2002.

preferably similarly to those that are illustrated in this chapter. The flash reports that are most informative are presented monthly (or weekly/daily) and give concise, yet significant, information as to the practice's performance. The dashboard reports should be prepared on a monthly basis. Finally, the more detailed reports, those that are part of dashboard reporting and the overall annual reporting at year-end, should be completed.

Successful medical practice operations are not accidentally achieved. Success requires competent and highly credentialed providers. Knowledgeable staff that are well-trained and work as a team are indispensable. Compliance with regulatory requirements and constant monitoring of these matters are essential. The establishment of well-defined policies and procedures is also important. An information system that provides accurate and quality data is an absolute. With all of these things in mind, however, without the implementation and utilization of sound financial data, which eventually transcends to good interpretation, the success of the practice will be limited.

This book illustrates the various ways to formulate a well-managed practice from the financial point of view. While certainly this is not the only ingredient to a successful practice, it is one of the most important. Maximizing revenue while controlling expenses is a simplistic way of summarizing sound financial management. Clearly, there are more issues involved in order to realizing these results, but this book attempts to illustrate those integral parts that form the basis of sound financial management.

Like most issues in business, financial management has certain constants as well as many variables. As the manager and physician-owner continue to improve in their ability to operate a successful medical practice or other health care entity, it is essential to continue to grow in areas of financial management.

Financial Language

Because financial analysis and financial statement relationships include an understanding of not only the numbers that make up the reports, but also the terminologies, this Glossary summarizes the financial language and terms that are pertinent to the medical practice.

A

Account Payable   A *liability* representing an amount owed to a *creditor*, usually arising from the purchase of *merchandise* or materials and supplies, not necessarily due or past due. Normally, a current liability, arising from the day-to-day operation of the business.

Account Receivable   A claim against a *debtor*, usually arising from sales or services rendered, not necessarily due or past due. Normally, a *current* asset, arising from the normal course of business.

Accounting   A service activity whose function is to provide quantitative information, primarily financial in nature, about economic entities. This service is intended to be useful in making economic decisions.

Accounting Equation   *Assets = Liabilities + Owners' Equity.*

Accounting Period   The time period for which *financial statements* that measure *flows*, such as the *income statement* and the *statement of cash flows*, are prepared. This period should be clearly defined on the financial statements. Normally, for no less than one month and no more than one year.

Accounting System   The procedures for collecting and summarizing financial data in a firm.

Accounts Receivable Turnover   Net *sales* on account divided by average *accounts receivable*. See *ratio*.

Accrual Basis of Accounting   The method of recognizing *revenue* as goods are sold (or delivered) and as services are rendered, independent of the time when cash is received. *Expenses* are recognized in the period when the related revenue is recognized independent of the time when cash is paid out.

Acquisition Cost   Of an *asset*, the net *invoice* price plus all *expenditures* to place and ready the asset for its intended use. The other expenditures might include legal fees, transportation charges, and installation costs.

Adjusted Bank Balance of Cash   The *balance* shown on the statement from the bank, plus or minus amounts such as for unrecorded deposits or outstanding checks, used to reconcile the bank's balance with the correct cash balance.

Adjusted Book Balance of Cash   The *balance* shown in the firm's account for cash in bank, plus or minus amounts such as for *notes* collected by the bank or bank service charges, used to reconcile the account balance with the correct cash balance.

Adjusting Entry   An entry made at the end of an *accounting period* to record a *transaction* or other *accounting event*, which for some reason has not been recorded or has been improperly recorded during the accounting period. An entry to update the accounts.

Administrative Expense   An *expense* related to the enterprise as a whole as contrasted to expenses related to more specific functions.

Admission of Partner   Legally, when a new partner joins a *partnership*, the old partnership is dissolved and a new one comes into being. In practice, however, the old accounting records may be kept in use and the accounting entries reflect the manner in which the new partner joined the firm. If the new partner merely purchases the interest of another partner, the only accounting is to change the name for one capital account. If the new partner contributes *assets* and *liabilities* to the partnership, the new assets must be recognized with debits and the liabilities and other source of capital, with credits.

Aging Accounts Receivable   The process of classifying *accounts receivable* by the time elapsed since the claim came into existence for the purpose of estimating the amount of uncollectible accounts receivable as of a given date. It is also a management tool to determine wherein emphasis should be placed in order to complete collection of certain accounts receivable.

Allocate   To spread a *cost* from one *account* to several accounts, to several products or activities, to several periods, or to several cost centers. Would also apply to revenue in the same manner.

Americans with Disabilities Act (ADA)   The federal law that governs the rights of individuals with physical disabilities.

Amortization   The process of liquidating or extinguishing ("bring of death") a *debt* with a series of payments to the *creditor* (or to a *sinking fund*). From that usage, a related use has evolved, which involves the accounting for the payments themselves: "amortization schedule" for a mortgage, which is a table showing the allocation between *interest* and *principle*. The term has come to mean writing off (ie, liquidating) the cost of an asset. In this context, it means the general process of *allocating acquisition* cost of an asset to either the periods of benefit as *expenses* or *inventory* accounts a *product costs*.

Appraisal   The process of obtaining a valuation for an *asset* or *liability* that involves expert opinion rather than evaluation of explicit market transactions.

Appreciation   An increase in economic worth caused by rising market prices for an asset.

Arm's Length   Said of a transaction negotiated by unrelated parties, each acting in his or her own self-interest; the basis for a *fair market value* determination.

Articles of Incorporation   Document filed with state authorities by persons forming a corporation. When the document is returned with a certificate of incorporation, it becomes the corporation's *charter*.

Assess   Defined as probable future economic benefits obtained or controlled by a particular entity as a result of past transactions.

Assignment of Accounts Receivable   Transfer of the legal ownership of an *account receivable* through its sale.

Audit   Systematic inspection of accounting records involving analyses, tests, and *confirmations*. See *internal audit*.

B

Bad Debt   An uncollectible *account receivable*.

Bad Debt Recovery   Collection, perhaps partial, of a specific account receivable that was previously written off as uncollectible.

Balance   As a noun, the sum of *debit* entries minus the sum of *credit* entries in an account.

Balance Sheet   Statement of financial position that shows *Total Assets* = Total Liabilities + Owners' Equity.

Balloon   Most *mortgage* and *installment loans* require relatively equal periodic payments. Sometimes, the loan requires relatively equal periodic payments with a large final payment. The large final payment is called a *balloon* payment. Such loans are called *balloon loans*.

Bank Balance   The amount of the balance in a checking account, shown on the *bank statement*.

Bank Reconciliation Schedule   A schedule that shows the difference between the book balance of the cash in a bank account and the bank's statement. This schedule takes into account the amount of such items as checks issued that have not cleared, deposits that have not cleared, deposits that have not been recorded by the bank, as well as errors made by the bank or the firm.

Bank Statement   A statement sent by the bank to a checking account customer that shows deposits, checks cleared, and service charges for a period, usually one month.

Bankrupt   Said of a company whose *liabilities* exceed its assets where a legal petition has been filed and accepted under the bankruptcy law. A bankrupt firm is usually, but need not be, insolvent.

Bill   An *invoice* of charges and *terms of sale* for goods and services. A bill is also a piece of currency.

Bonus   Premium over normal *wage* or *salary*; usually paid for meritorious performance.

Book   As a verb, to record a transaction to the formal accounting records. As a noun, usually plural, the *journals* and *ledgers*. As an adjective, see *book value*.

Book Value   The amount shown in the books or in the accounts for an *asset, liability,* or *owners' equity* item. Generally used to refer to the *net* amount of an *asset* or group of assets shown in the account, which records the asset and reductions, such as for *amortization*, in its cost. With a firm, the excess of total assets over total liabilities. See *net assets*.

Branch   A sales office or other unit of an enterprise that is physically separated from the home office of the enterprise, but not organized as a legally separate *subsidiary*.

Breakeven Point   The volume of sales required so that total *revenues* and total *costs* are equal.

Budget   A financial plan that is used to estimate the results of future operations. Frequently used to control future operations.

Burn Rate   A new business usually begins life with cash-absorbing operating losses, but with a limited amount of cash. The "burn rate" measures how long the new business can survive before operating losses must stop or a new infusion of cash will be necessary. The measurement is ordinarily stated in terms of months.

Bylaws   The rules adopted by the shareholders of a corporation that specify the general methods for carrying out the functions of the corporation.

C

Capital   *Owners' equity* in a business. Often used, with equal accuracy, to mean the total assets of a business. Sometimes used to mean *capital assets*.

Capital Asset   Properly used, capital assets are the designation for income tax purposes that describes property that is held by a taxpayer, except cash, inventorial assets, goods (held primarily for sale), most depreciable property, *real estate, receivables,* certain *intangibles,* and a few other items.

Capital Budget   Plan of proposed outlays for acquiring long-term *assets* and the means of *financing* the acquisition.

Capital Gain   The excess of proceeds over *cost,* or other *basis,* from the sale of a *capital asset* as defined by the Internal Revenue Code. If the capital asset has been held for a sufficiently long period of time before sale, then the tax on the gain is computed at a rate lower than is used for other gains and ordinary income.

Capital Lease   A lease treated by the *lessee* as both the borrowing of funds and the acquisition of an asset to be *amortized.* Both the *liability* and the asset are recognized on the balance sheet. Expenses consist of *interest* on the *debt* and *amortization/depreciation* of the asset. The *lessor* treats the lease as the sale of the asset in return for a series of future cash receipts. Contrast with *operating lease.*

Capitalization of Earnings   The process of estimating the economic worth of a firm by computing the net present value of the predicted *net income* (not *cash flows*) of the firm for the future.

Cash   Currency and coins, negotiable checks, and balances in bank accounts. For the *statement of cash flows,* cash also includes *marketable securities* held as current assets.

Cash Basis of Accounting   In contrast to the *accrual basis of accounting,* a system of accounting in which *revenues* are recognized when cash is received and *expenses* are recognized as *disbursements* are made. No attempt is made to *match revenues* and *expenses* in determining *income.*

Cash Budget   Schedule of expected cash *receipts* and *disbursements.*

Cash Flow   Cash *receipts,* minus *disbursements,* from a given *asset,* or group of assets, for a given period.

Cash Receipts Journal   A specialized *journal* used to record all *receipts* of cash.

Certified Check   The check from a depositor that is drawn from a bank. On the face of the check, the bank has inserted the words *accepted* or *certified,* and include the date and signature of a bank official. The check then becomes an obligation of the bank. Compares with *cashier's check.*

Chart of Accounts   A systematically organized list of names and numbers of *accounts.* The General Ledger is formulated from this basic listing.

Check   The Federal Reserve Board defines a check as "a *draft* or order upon a bank or banking house purporting to be drawn upon a deposit of funds for the payment at all events of a certain sum of money to a certain person therein named or to him or his order or to bearer and payable instantly on demand." It must contain the phrase "pay to the order of." The amount shown on the check's face must be clearly readable and it must have the signature of the drawer. Checks need not be dated, although they usually are. The *balance* in the *cash account* is usually reduced when a check is issued, not later when it clears the bank and reduces cash in bank.

Check Register   A *journal* to record *checks* that are issued.

Close   As a verb, to transfer the balance of a *temporary* or *contra* or *adjunct* account to the main account to which it relates (eg, to transfer *revenue* and *expense* accounts directly, or through the *income summary,* to an *owners' equity* account, or to transfer *purchase discounts* to purchases). To *close* the books entails the above, usually done only once each year, at the end of the fiscal year.

Closing Entries   The *entries* that accomplish the transfer of balances in *temporary accounts* to the related *balance sheet accounts.*

Coinsurance   Insurance policies that protect against hazards, such as fire or water damage, and often specify that the owner of the property may not collect the full amount of insurance for a loss unless the insurance policy covers at least some specified *coinsurance* percentage, usually about 80% of the *replacement cost* of the property. Coinsurance clauses induce the owner to carry full, or nearly full, coverage.

COLA   Cost-of-living adjustment. See *indexation.*

Collateral   *Assets* pledged by a *borrower* that will be given up if the *loan* is not paid.

Collectible   Capable of being converted into *cash*; now, if due; later, otherwise.

Commercial Paper   *Short-term notes* issued by corporate borrowers.

Commission   Remuneration, usually expressed as a percentage, to employees, based upon an activity rate, such as sales.

Comparative (Financial) Statements   *Financial statements* showing information for the same company for different times, usually two successive years. Nearly all published financial statements are in this form. Contrast with *historical summary*.

Compound Interest   Interest calculated on *principal* plus previously undistributed interest.

Consolidated Financial Statements   Statements issued by legally separate companies, but common ownership, that show financial position and income as they would appear if the companies were one economic *entity*.

Control System   A device for ensuring that actions are carried out according to plan or for safeguarding *assets*. A system for ensuring that actions are carried out according to plan; can be designed: for a single function within the firm, called *operational control*; for autonomous segments within the firm that generally have responsibility for both revenues and costs, called *divisional control*; or for activities of the firm as a whole, called *company-wide control*. Systems designed for safeguarding *assets* are called *internal control* systems.

Controller   The title often used for the chief accountant of an organization. Often spelled *comptroller*.

Corporation   A legal entity authorized by a state to operate under the rules of the entity's *charter*.

Correcting Entry   An *adjusting entry* where an improperly recorded *transaction* is properly recorded. Not to be confused with entries that correct *accounting errors*.

Cost   The sacrifice, measured by the *price* paid or required to be paid, to acquire *goods* or *services*.

Cost Center   A unit of activity for which *expenditures* and *expenses* are accumulated.

Credit   As a noun, an entry on the right-hand side of an account. As a verb, to make an entry on the right-hand side of an account. Records increases in *liabilities, owner's equity, revenues*, and *gains*; records decreases in assets and expenses. See *debit and credit conventions*. Also the ability or right to buy or borrow in return for a promise to pay later.

Credit Memorandum   A document used by a seller to inform a buyer that the buyer's *account receivable* is being credited (reduced) because of *errors, returns*, or *allowances*. Also, the document provided by a bank to a depositor to indicate that the depositor's

balance is being increased because of some event other than a deposit, such as the collection by the bank of the depositor's *note receivable*.

Current Asset   *Cash* and other *assets* that are expected to be turned into cash, sold, or exchanged within the normal operating cycle of the firm, usually one year. Current *assets* include *cash, marketable securities, receivable, inventory*, and *current prepayments*.

Current Funds   *Cash* and other assets readily convertible into cash.

Current Liability   A debt or other obligation that must be discharged within a short time, usually the *earnings cycle* or one year, normally by expending *current assets*.

Current Replacement Cost   Of an *asset*, the amount currently required to acquire an identical asset (in the same condition and with the same service potential) or an asset capable of rendering the same service at a current *fair market price*.

Customers' Ledger   The *ledger* that shows accounts receivable of individual customers. It is the *subsidiary ledger* for the *controlling account*, Accounts Receivable.

D

Debit   As a noun, an entry on the left-hand side of an *account*. As a verb, to make an entry on the left-hand side of an account. Records increases in *assets* and *expenses*; records decreases in *liabilities, owners' equity*, and *revenues*.

Debit Memorandum   A document used by a seller to inform a buyer that the seller is debiting (increasing) the amount of the buyer's *account receivable*. Also, the document provided by a bank to a depositor to indicate that the depositor's *balance* is being decreased because of some event other than payment for a *check*, such as monthly service charges or the printing of checks.

Debt   An amount owed. The general name for *notes, bonds, mortgages*, and the like that are evidence of amounts owed and have definite payment dates.

Deferral   The accounting process concerned with past *cash receipts* and *payments*; in contrast to *accrual*. Recognizing a liability resulting from a current cash receipt (as for magazines to be delivered) or recognizing an asset from a current cash payment (or for prepaid insurance or a long-term depreciable asset).

Defined Contribution Plan   A *money purchase (pension) plan* or other arrangement, based on formula or discretion, where the employer makes cash contributions to eligible individual employee *accounts* under the terms of a written plan document (eg, profit-sharing pension plans).

Depreciation *Amortization of capital assets*; the process of allocating the cost of an asset to the periods of benefit—*the depreciable life*. Classified as a *production cost* or a *period expense*, depending upon the asset and whether *absorption* or *variable costing* is used.

Disbursement Payment by *cash* or by *check*.

Double Entry The system of recording transactions that maintains the equality of the accounting equation; each entry results in recording equal amounts of *debits* and *credits*.

E

Endorsement See *draft*. The *payee* signs the draft and transfers it to a fourth party, such as the payee's bank.

Equity A claim to *assets*; a source of assets.

ERISA Employment Retirement Income Security Act of 1974. The federal law that sets most *pension plan* requirements.

Expense As a noun, a decrease in *owners' equity* caused by the using up of *assets* in producing *revenue* or carrying out other activities that are part of the entity's *operations*.

F

Fair Market Price (Value) Price (value) negotiated at *arm's length* between a willing buyer and a willing seller, each acting rationally in his or her own self-interest. May be estimated in the absence of a monetary transaction.

FICA Federal Insurance Contributions Act. The law that sets *Social Security* taxes and benefits. Also includes Medicare taxes as a portion thereof.

Financial Projection An estimate of *financial position*, results of *operations*, and changes in cash flows for one or more periods based on a set of assumptions. If the assumptions are not necessarily the most likely outcomes, then the estimate is called a *projection*. If the assumptions represent the most probable outcomes, then the estimate is called a *forecast*. *Most probable* means that the assumptions have been evaluated by management and that they are management's judgment of the most likely set of conditions and most likely outcomes. Statement of the *assets* and *equities* of a firm are displayed as a *balance sheet*.

Financial Statements The *balance sheet, income statement, statement of retained earnings, statement of cash flows,* statement of changes of *owners' equity* accounts, and *notes* thereto.

Fiscal Year A period of 12 consecutive months chosen by a business as the *accounting period* for annual reports. May or may not be a *natural business year* or calendar year.

Fixed Cost (Expense) An *expenditure* or *expense* that does not vary with volume of activity, at least in the short run.

Float *Checks* whose amounts have been *added* to depositor's bank account, but not yet subtracted from the *drawer's* bank account.

Foreclosure The borrower fails to make a required payment on a *mortgage*; the lender takes possession of the property for his or her use or sale. Assume that the lender sells the property, but the proceeds of sale are insufficient to cover the outstanding balance on the loan at the time of foreclosure. Under the terms of most mortgages, the lender becomes an unsecured creditor of the borrower for the still unrecovered balance of the loan.

Fully Vested Said of a *pension plan* when an employee (or his or her estate) has rights to all the benefits purchased with the employer's contributions to the plan, even if the employee is not employed by this employer at the time of death or retirement.

FUTA The Federal Unemployment Tax Act provides for taxes to be collected at the federal level, in an effort to help subsidize the individual states' administration of their employment compensation programs.

G

General Journal The formal record where transactions, or summaries of similar transactions, are recorded in *journal entry* form as they occur. Use of the adjective *general* usually implies only two columns for cash amounts or that there are also various *special journals*, such as a *check register* or *sales journal*, in use.

General Ledger The name for the formal *ledger* containing all of the financial statement accounts.

Goodwill The excess of cost of an acquired firm (or operating unit) over the current *fair market value* of the separately identifiable *net assets* of the acquired unit. Before goodwill is recognized, all identifiable assets, whether on the books of the acquired unit or not, must be given a *fair market value*.

Grandfather Clause An exemption in new accounting *pronouncements* exempting transactions that occurred before a given date from the new accounting treatment.

Gross Not adjusted or reduced by deductions or subtractions. Contrast with *net*.

H

Holding Company A company that confines its activities to owning *stock* in, and supervising management of, other companies. A holding company usually owns a controlling interest, that being more than 50% of the voting stock, of the companies whose stock it holds.

I

Income   *Excess of revenues* and *gains* over *expenses* and *losses* for a period; *net income*. Sometimes used with an appropriate modifier to refer to the various intermediate amounts shown in a *multiple-step income statement*. Sometimes used to refer to revenues, as in *rental income*.

Income Accounts   *Revenue* and *expense accounts*.

Income Statement   The statement of *revenues, expenses, gains,* and *losses* for the period, ending with *net income* for the period.

Income Tax   An annual tax levied by the federal and other governments on the income of an entity.

Indexation   An attempt by lawmakers or parties of a contract to cope with the effects of *inflation*. Amounts fixed in law or contracts are *indexed* when they change as a given measure of price changes.

Inflation   A time of generally rising prices.

Information System   A system, either formal or informal, for collecting, processing, and communicating data that are useful for the managerial functions of decision making, planning, and controlling, and are used for financial reporting.

Installment   Partial payment of a debt or collection of a receivable, usually according to a contract.

Insurance   A contract for reimbursement of specific losses, purchased with insurance premiums. Self-insurance is not insurance, but merely the willingness to assume risk of incurring losses while saving the premium.

Intangible Asset   A nonphysical, *noncurrent* right that gives a firm an exclusive or preferred position in the marketplace. Examples are a *copyright, patent, trademark, goodwill, organization costs, capitalized* advertising costs, computer programs, licenses for any of the preceding, government licenses, leases, franchises, mailing lists, exploration permits, import and export permits, construction permits, and marketing quotas.

Interest   The charge or cost for using money; expressed as a rate per period, usually one year, call the *interest rate*.

Internal Audit   An *audit* conducted by employees to ascertain whether or not *internal control* procedures are working. An external audit is conducted by a certified public accountant.

Internal Revenue Service (IRS)   Agency of the US Treasury Department responsible for administering the Internal Revenue Code and collecting income and certain other taxes.

In the Black (Red)   Operating at a profit (loss).

Inventory   As a noun, the *balance* in an asset *account*, such as raw materials, supplies, work in process, and finished goods. As a verb, to calculate the *cost* of goods on hand at a given time or to physically count items on hand.

Investment   An *expenditure* to acquire property or other assets in order to produce *revenue*; the *asset* so acquired; a *current* expenditure made in anticipation of future income.

J

Journal   The place where transactions are recorded as they occur. The book of original entry.

Journal Entry   A recording in a *journal*, of equal *debits* and *credits*, with an explanation of the transaction, *if necessary*.

K

Kiting   This term means slightly different things in banking and auditing contexts. In both, however, it refers to the wrongful practice of taking advantage of the *float*, the time that elapses between the deposit of a *check* in one bank and its collection at another.

L

Lapping (Accounts Receivable)   The theft, by an employee, of cash sent in by a customer to discharge the latter's *payable*. The theft from the first customer is concealed by using cash received from a second customer. The theft from the second customer is concealed by using the cash received from a third customer, and so on. The process is continued until the thief returns the funds or can make the theft permanent by creating a fictitious *expense* or receivable write-off, or until the fraud is discovered.

Lease

A contract calling for the lessee (user) to pay the lessor (owner) for the use of an asset.

Leasehold Improvement

An *improvement* to leased property. Should be *amortized* over *service life* or the life of the lease, whichever is shorter.

Ledger   A book of accounts.

Liability   An obligation to pay a definite (or reasonably definite) amount at a definite (or reasonably definite) time in return for a past or current benefit. A liability has three essential characteristics: (1) an obligation to transfer assets or services at a specified or determinable date, (2) the entity has little or no discretion to avoid the transfer, and (3) the event causing the obligation has already happened (ie, it is not executory).

Limited Partner   Member of a *partnership* not personally liable for debts of the partnership; every partnership must have at least one *general partner* who is fully liable.

Liquid Assets   *Cash, current marketable securities, and, sometimes, current receivables.*

Loan   An arrangement where the owner of property, called the lender, allows someone else, called the borrower, the use of the property for a period of time that is usually specified in the agreement setting up the loan. The borrower promises to return the property to the lender and, often, to make a payment for the use of the property. Generally used when the property is *cash* and the payment for its use is *interest.*

Loss   Excess of cost over net proceeds for a single transaction; negative *income* for a period. A cost expiration that produced no *revenue.*

M

Margin   *Revenue,* less specified expenses.

Merger   The joining of two or more businesses into a single *economic entity.* See *holding company.*

Mortgage   A claim given by the borrower (mortgage) against the borrower's property in return for a loan.

N

Negotiable   Legally capable of being transferred by endorsement. Usually said of *checks* and *notes* and sometimes of *stocks* and *bearer bonds.*

Net   Reduced by all relevant deductions.

Net Income   The excess of all *expenses* and *gains* for a period over all *expenses* and *losses* of that same period.

Net Loss   The excess of all *expenses* and *losses* for a period over all *revenues* and *gains* of that same period.

Nonprofit Corporation   An incorporated *entity,* such as a hospital, with owners who do not share in the earnings. It usually emphasizes providing services rather than maximizing income.

Note   An unconditional written promise by the maker (borrower) to pay a certain amount on demand or at a certain future time.

O

OASD(H)I   *Old Age, Survivors, Disability, and (Hospital) Insurance.*

Operating   An adjective used to refer to *revenue* and *expense items* relating to the company's *main line(s) of business.*

OSHA   Occupational Safety and Health Act. The federal law that governs working conditions in commerce and industry.

Out-of-Pocket   Said of an *expenditure* usually paid for with cash. An *incremental* cost.

Outstanding   Unpaid or uncollected. When said of a check, it means a check issued that did not clear the *drawer's* bank prior to the *bank statement* due.

Overdraft   A check written on a checking account that contains funds less than the amount of the check.

Overhead Costs   Any cost not directly associated with the production or sale of identifiable goods and services.

P

P & L   Profit and loss statement, *income statement.*

Partnership   Contractual arrangement between individuals to share resources and operations in a jointly run business.

Payable   Unpaid, but not necessarily due or past due.

Payroll Taxes   Taxes levied because salaries or wages are paid (eg, FICA, unemployment compensation insurance taxes). Typically, the employer pays a portion and withholds part of the employee's wage fund.

Pension Fund   *Fund,* the assets of which are to be paid to retired, ex-employees—usually as a *life annuity.* This fund is typically held by an independent trustee and thus is not an *asset* of the employer.

Pension Plan   Details or provisions of an employer's contract with employees for paying retirement *annuities* or other benefits.

Petty Cash Fund   Currency and coins maintained for expenditures that are made with cash on hand.

Prime Rate   The rate for loans charged by commercial banks to their creditworthy customers.

Principal   An amount in which *interest* is charged or earned. The *face amount of a loan.* Also, the absent owner (principal) who hires the manager or accountant (agent) in a *principal-agent* relationship.

Prior-Period Adjustment   A *debit* or *credit* made directly to *retained earnings* (that does not affect income for the period) to adjust earnings as calculated for prior periods.

Pro Forma Statements   Hypothetical statements. Financial statements as they would appear if some event, such as a *merger* or increased production and sales, had occurred or were to occur. Pro forma is often spelled as one word.

Profit Center   A unit of activity for which either revenue or *expenses* are accumulated; contrast with *cost center.*

Profit Sharing Plan   A *defined contribution plan,* where the employer contributes amounts based on net *income.*

Promissory Note An unconditional written promise to pay a specified sum of money on demand or at a specified date.

Prorate To *allocate* in proportion to some base.

Purchase Order Document authorizing a seller to deliver goods with the payment to be made later.

R

Ratio The number resulting when one number is divided by another. Ratios are generally used to assess aspects of profitability, solvency, and liquidity. The three commonly used financial ratios are: (1) those that summarize some aspect of *operations* for a period, usually a year; (2) those that summarize some aspect of *financial position* at a given moment—the moment for which a balance sheet has been prepared; and (3) those that relate some aspect of operations to some aspect of financial position.

Receipt Acquisition of *cash.*

Rent A charge for the use of land, buildings, or other assets.

Retained Earnings Net *income* over the life of a corporation, less all *dividends* (including capitalization through *stock dividends*); *owners' equity less contributed capital.*

Revenue The increase in *owners' equity* caused by a service rendered or the sale of goods. The monetary measure of a service rendered.

Risk A measure of a variability of the *return on investment.* For a given expected amount of return, most people prefer less risk to more risk. Therefore, in national markets, investments with more risk usually promise, or are expected to yield, a higher rate of return than investments with lower risk. Most people use *risk* and *uncertainty* as synonyms. In technical language, however, these terms have different meanings. Risk is used when the probabilities attached to the various outcomes are known, such as the probabilities of heads or tails in the flip of a fair coin. Uncertainty refers to an event where the probabilities of the outcomes, such as winning or losing a lawsuit, can only be estimated.

Risk Premium Extra compensation paid to an employee or extra *interest* paid to a lender, over the amounts usually considered normal, in return for their undertaking to engage in activities more risky than normal.

ROI *Return on investment,* but usually used to refer to a single project and expressed as a ration; *income* divided by the average *cost* of *assets* devoted to the project.

S

Salary Compensation that is earned by the manager, administration, or professional, not based on an hourly rate. Contrast with *wage.*

Sale A *revenue* transaction where *goods* or *services* are delivered to a customer in return for cash or a contractual obligation to pay.

Simple Interest *Interest* calculated on *principal* where interest earned during periods before maturity of the loan is neither added to the principal nor paid to the lender. *Interest = principal × interest rate × time.* Seldom used in economic calculations, except for periods less than one year. Contrast with *compound interest.*

Social Security Taxes Taxes levied by the federal government on both employers and employees to provide *funds* to pay retired persons (or their survivors) who are entitled to receive such payments, either because they paid Social Security taxes themselves or because the Congress has declared them eligible.

Sole Proprietorship All *owners' equity* belongs to one person.

Spread Sheet A *worksheet* organized like a *matrix* that provides a two-way classification of accounting data.

T

T-Account Account form shaped like the letter T with the title above the horizontal line. *Debits* are shown to the left of the vertical line, *credits* to the right.

Take-Home Pay The amount of a paycheck; earned wages or *salary, minus* the deductions for *income taxes, social security taxes,* contributions to fringe benefit plans, union dues, and so on.

Tax Credit A subtraction from taxes that are otherwise payable. Contrast with *tax deduction.*

Tax Deduction A subtraction from *revenues* and *gains* to arrive at taxable income. Tax deductions are technically different from tax *exemptions,* but the effect of both is to reduce gross income in computing taxable income. Both are different from *tax credits,* which are subtracted.

Taxable Income *Income* that is computed according to IRS regulation and subject to *income taxes.* Contrast with income, net income, income before taxes (in the *income statement*), and *comprehensive income (a financial reporting* concept). Use the term *pretax income* to refer to income before taxes on the income statement in financial reports.

Tickler File A collection of *vouchers* or other memoranda arranged chronologically to remind the person in charge of certain duties to make payments (or to do other tasks) as scheduled.

Trial Balance A listing of *account balances*: all accounts with *debit* balances are totaled separately from accounts with *credit* balances. The two totals should be equal. Trial balances are taken as a partial check of the arithmetic accuracy of the entries that were previously made.

U

Underwriter One who agrees to purchase an entire *security issue* for a specified price, usually for resale to others.

V

Value Monetary worth; the term is usually so subjective that it ought not to be used without a modifying adjective, unless most people would agree on the amount. Not to be confused with cost. See *fair market value*.

Variance Difference between actual and *standard costs* or between *budgeted* and actual *expenditures* or, sometimes, *expenses*.

Vendor A seller.

Vested Said of an employee's *pension plan* benefits that are not contingent on the employee's continued employment for the employer.

W

Wage Employee compensation based on time worked or output of product for manual labor. See *take-home pay*.

Warranty A promise by a seller to correct deficiencies in products sold.

Weighted Average An average computed by counting each occurrence of each value, not merely a single occurrence of each value.

Withholding Deductions from *salaries* or *wages*, usually for *income taxes*, to be remitted by the employer, in the employee's name, to the taxing authority.

Write Down A *write off* with all of the asset's cost charged to expense or *loss*. Generally used for nonrecurring items.

Write Off To *charge* an asset to *expense* or *loss* (ie, *debit* expense [or loss], *credit* asset).

Page numbers in **bold** refer to glossary terms.

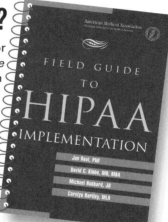

Improve your
bottom line

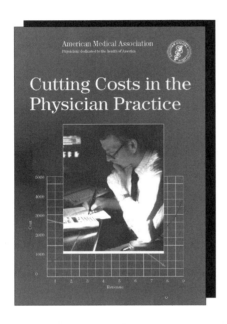

Cutting Costs in the Physician Practice

Looking for ways to stay on top of your bottom line?

Cutting Costs in the Physician Practice *helps you identify and implement cost-cutting measures that ultimately increase your profits.*

Cutting Costs in the Physician Practice

With the explosion of managed care, even the most successful practices must control costs effectively to stay financially healthy. Written by experienced consultants, this book provides practical advice and solutions that have proven successful in medical practices. It identifies key areas within health care practices where costs most often get out of control. Armed with this knowledge, physicians can better put their resources to work — building a stronger, more financially secure practice.

Order #: OP068600
Price: $55.00
AMA Member Price: $50.00

Phone orders: (800) 621-8335   **Secured online orders: www.amapress.com**

VISA, MasterCard, American Express and Optima accepted. State sales tax and shipping/handling charges apply.
Satisfaction guaranteed or return within 30 days for full refund.

American Medical Association
Physicians dedicated to the health of America

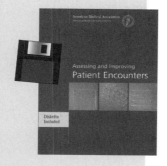

00AD04

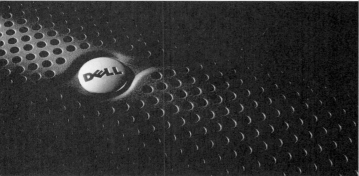